All things resist being written down
Kafka Diaries, 1913

Also by Rosemary Dinnage:

Annie Besant
One to One: Experiences of Psychotherapy
The Ruffian on the Stair: Reflection on Death
Alone! Alone! Lives of Outsider Women

The Long Vacation

Rosemary Dinnage

Brook Green

© Rosemary Dinnage, 2012

ISBN 978-1-4717-4012-1

Brook Green

Acknowledgments

With gratitude to John Ryle and Toby Collins, without whom I would have never have finished this book, at a difficult time. And to my two sons, Simon and Mark, who designed and advised.

Contents

Introduction   p. 1

PART I

    1. Rhodes House   p. 15
    2. Leaving home   p. 69
    3. And coming back   p. 113

PART II

    4. Psychoanalysis   p. 147
    5. Exploring   p. 163
    6. Ending Up   p. 197

Fragments   p. 213

Bibliography   p. 217

Introduction

I was with a few friends, doing the tourist visit to Bletchley Park, where the great decoders of the Second World War worked – empty sheds, dusty machines, echoing absence of the clatter and tension that were once here. In the café we chanced upon Dr Anthony Kenny, then Warden of Rhodes House, that monumental centre for Oxford's Rhodes Scholars. It has libraries, lecture rooms, subterranean storerooms, and one luxurious wing is called the Warden's Lodging. 'That's where I grew up!', I piped, and Dr Kenny and I embarked on a Rhodes House miscellany: the boringness of the constantly visiting Trustees, the clatter and smell of cigars wafting up to the nursery, the hierarchy of 1930s servants (white aprons, frilled caps), the wickedness of sliding down the lovely curved banisters, the feuding governesses and gardeners. I was awfully cheeky.

'You ought to write it all down,' said kindly Dr Kenny. 'Quite a story!' And, some years ago, I did.

Then I moved house, lost manuscripts, spent time with plumbers and electricians, pushed boxes into cupboards, stacked bookshelves, lost and found things many times over, and eventually under a pile of school reports, found a substantial chunk of manuscript. I'd titled it *The Long Vacation.*

Why? I'd found as I wrote that the Rhodes House life, in spite of its upper-class gloss, meant many separations for children: long parental vacations spent on Rhodes House business or just 'recharging the batteries', nannies that came and went, uneasy stays with Granny, more loneliness than I'd wanted to remember, in the gaps between family times.

The manuscript seemed to add up, at the most, to about 30,000 words. I'd worked enough as a journalist to know that this wasn't long enough for a book; I was confused, too, about the difference between a 'memoir' and an autobiography. The latter, I felt, was what important pop stars and politicians wrote. But still... mightn't some reader, after finishing the childhood, have wondered what happened to her later?

Rightly or wrongly, I decided to go on, to condense some sixty years into – let's say – a few more short chapters. There was a huge stack of diary notebooks. Ancestral voices were calling out phrases well known to English children of my generation: 'You're not the only pebble on the beach'; 'No more *me*'; 'We don't want to hear about that, thank you'. I ignored them.

There was surely a pattern, a sequence, a linking that held fragments together. I've always been inquisitive and I wanted to find it.

PART I

THE LONG VACATION

1. *Rhodes House*

THE LONG VACATION

(i)

'Have you done your duty today?'

In 1902, after increasing illness, Cecil John Rhodes died at the age of 48 in a cottage near Cape Town in South Africa. The whole British Empire, it was said, was in mourning. Tributes to the 'Colossus of Africa' poured in from all over the world.

Bells tolled, flags hung at half-mast for the man who understood 'the imperial destinies of the British race'. During his funeral journey across Africa, crowds filled the station platforms and bands played slow music. His coffin was hauled up by a team of oxen to his chosen mountain grave and buried beneath a granite slab. It is not much visited now. Rhodes's last words were reported to have been 'So little done, so much to do'; noble, but a more reliable source gives them as, 'Turn me over, Jack.' At the time my mother was four years old, youngest child of Edward and Jane Halford living in Oxford, my father the 14-year-old son of a clergyman in Sydney, Australia.

* * * *

I should have been born in Oxford, but my parents, a don and his wife, had lost their first child at birth and for safety's sake I was born in a well equipped nursing home overlooking Hyde Park. After a successful birth and the usual two weeks lying-in, she and I returned to our Oxford home, newly built in a north Oxford suburb and suitable for an academic and his family.

Some psychologists have said that there are no real memories before the age of three, some autobiographers claim memories from the pram; Sam Beckett notably remembered – with distaste – life in the womb. I do have a few, scanty memories of life in those first few years.

I firmly believe I remember screaming for food; something in me still screams. My mother was told (I suppose it was by a follower of the terrible New Zealand paediatrician Truby King) that if I cried for less than four hours a day my lungs wouldn't grow.

Next-door was where the Galbraith family lived. Next-door had a lavatory completely papered in yellow Fyffes-bananas stickers: this to me was the wonder of the world. I think that at the time (1930) bananas with their blue and yellow stickers were all shipped from the empire on the Fyffes' boats – now undercut by cheap and tasteless South American fruit. Here lived Jim, dear Jim who was a few months older than me. How much are early memories influenced by photographs? The misty one of Jim and me hand in hand still touches my heart. Has anyone since Jim looked at me with such devotion? If I had a second chance at life I might return it to the moment of that photo as a starting-point.

A sliver of silver tinsel belongs to that time, in a curious way. Some thirty years later, when I was trying out psychoanalysis, I felt impelled, somehow to bring a strip of tinsel to a session.

One of the reasons I was such an unsuccessful analysand, I now think, was that I expected instant understanding of anything I was trying to get across; misunderstanding seemed to instantly demolish any attempt to be myself, like a kick at a half-finished jigsaw.

This particular psychoanalyst was understandably irritated by my waving a piece of tinsel (it was mere 'resistance'), and I was consequently demolished. Why the tinsel? I didn't know. But when I was going through my father's letters some time ago I found – among letters from university colleagues, writers, obscure politicians – one from him to a brother in Australia saying something like 'I wish you could have seen my two-year-old in her silver fairy dress this Christmas!' So from across those years there is still just a gleam, and every Christmas I still feel both thrilled and wretched. Because once there was a *something*, and I can't quite re-find it.

My other Garford Road memory is the clearest. I think of it as the first real memory, significant for a lifetime, deeply thought over. I see this as set against a green beech hedge: at the top of the road; my mother is saying, with force, 'Do you know you cried so loudly yesterday that Mr Galbraith heard you *from Carfax?*' (Carfax is some miles from suburban north Oxford.) I took it for granted that she was always right and knew everything. But this left questions: am I the naughtiest girl in the world? Does anyone come if you cry? Have I misunderstood space and distance? Finally: Or does she *tell lies*? They still reverberate.

My relationship with my mother was to become almost tragically bad later and I haven't wanted to dwell on this. But sometimes it will out. So much care and affection; so badly spoiled. To this clear early memory I attribute a kind of obsessive wish to get at the truth of things, to study the borderline between imagination and 'fact'. Another anecdote, perhaps accusatory, crops up; this was said when I was being kept awake by my own children. 'You must do what I did. I told you that if you woke me up again, you would damage me and the baby. I said, if you cry, I'll shut you in the box-room. And you never cried again!' So the course of my life was set.

To that Carfax memory I also attribute an attraction towards things that aren't simple fact: dreams, legends, odd religions, startling hypotheses. I'm told I hung on to the belief in fairies and Father Christmas long after I should have let go, and to my own children I couldn't tell the Father Christmas fable – how could I lie to them and then disillusion them? I've enjoyed my years of membership of a psychical research society, because it is devoted to investigation of the fantasy/fact borderline. Telepathy, at any rate, certainly exists, I have learned from it, though usually in the context of disaster or death. The telepathy that I love is the Jane Eyre kind. Jane is foolishly about to throw in her lot with the insufferable missionary St John Rivers ('you are formed for labour, Jane, not for love') when she goes to the window, moonlight streaming in:

> I saw nothing but I heard a voice somewhere cry –
>
> 'Jane! Jane! Jane!' nothing more.
> 'Oh God ! what is it?' I gasped.

I might have said, 'Where is it?' for it did not seem in the room – nor in the house – nor in the garden; it did not come out of the air – nor from under the earth – nor, from overhead. And it was the voice of a human being – a known, loved, well-remembered voice – that of Edward Fairfax Rochester; and it spoke in pain and woe wildly, eerily, urgently.

'I am coming' – I cried. 'Wait for me!'

Wildly, eerily urgently: reader, I adore it. This is the true magic, when the child's cry is answered.

* * * *

The Garford Road house from which we removed in 1931 lies in the territory of Deep Memory: of little black and white photographs, hearsay, yellow Fyffes stickers, the ghost of a fierce dog, a glint of tinsel. The grandparents' Park Town house, to which my mother and we two children temporarily moved during a journey of my father's, is also in north Oxford – a beautiful part – but as we were to be there so often over the years, it belongs to real memory. Even so, there is blurring: I was astonished to realise later that my grandmother's death was not until 1938, when I was eleven and it was just before the Second World War. When I was evacuated overseas during that war, everyone at home, somehow, seemed to die; so I got confused about real deaths. But still... the blurring? Was she loved? Feared? Distant? Close? To an aunt (by marriage) she seemed a termagant; to my mother, someone unbearably close, charged with (to me) baffling emotions.

Only the house still stands out clearly, with its Regency verandah overlooking garden and tall chestnut trees that made bonfires in autumn. I had stayed there first when I was around two, during the first of my parents' unbearable absences on holiday. A sole photo from that time shows a pretty scared-looking child in a pretty large armchair. Grandfather, I think, died not long after that, and stays in memory just for a few baffling sayings, 'Nobody knows what my nose knows'; *Tempus fugit'* (over and over again).

It must have been soon after this that I had another surprise from the baffling grown-ups. I was brought up to London to have my *proper* photograph taken by a rather grand photographer – the name I think, Marcus Adams. I sat up looking polite in a chair; there was some chatting; I was given a glass ball to hold, I wondered when I would have my picture taken. My mother was putting on her coat, the one with the dead, snarling fox round the neck; 'It's over, it's done', she cried. I was amazed. But in my spare room is the nicely framed evidence, in a white crepe-de-chine frock and with curls smoothed down. Delicately tinted in pastel tones, of course. There was no colour photography in 1931.

My grandmother, mother of six, was small and I think still rather pretty, and – even to childish eyes – deeply old-fashioned. She would have been about seventy when I was born. In the 1930s, she was still wearing skirts to the ankles and large black dome-shaped hats (even on the beach if she was with us on holiday, according to photographs.) But the house... The house (still there, of course) is clearest.

Thirty-six Park Town must be worth quite a lot of money now. How would the grandparents ever have imagined that? When they moved in to it in 1901, it would have seemed a decent sort of house for an Inland Revenue employee with wife and family. It is set among early Victorian terraces and faces a garden square to which the key must have been rarely granted, for I never saw anyone in it. The house had a gravelled front garden with of course, a bicycle shed – who could be without that in north Oxford? – and steps up to the front door. When opened, this revealed a seriously ugly piece of furniture combining mirror and umbrella stand, and one breathed in the special 'Granny's house' smell. Many, many jugs of over-boiled gravy were in the smell, and stacks of dusty boys' magazines from the 1890s, and damp seeping up from an unused cellar. The dining room, at the front, was especially gravy-imbued and portentous due, I suspect, to some gloomy family meals. My mother always declared she had an idyllic childhood, but my beloved Aunt Anne told a different story, of a tetchy and jealous head of household who sometimes refused to speak to the family for days at a time.

As far as I know, there was no one in my immediate ancestry on either side who had the habit of simply saying what they were feeling.

But the 'Granny's house' smell was... well, in a way rather delicious! And the L-shaped sitting-room at the back faced south and was lighter and brighter. This room had blue and white striped wallpaper, a grandfather clock, a piano which I seldom heard played but which indicated culture, narrow shelves of china ornaments all declaring 'A Present from Whitby' (or Southsea or Corfe Castle), many bound volumes of *Punch* – and a radiogram. In here the tea tray with its unstable silver jug would be set out on a gate-leg oak table, and a coal fire encouraged with bellows and poker.

Ancestry on this side of the family was, sadly, entirely undistinguished and respectable. My grandparents may originally have been from the Worcester area, though they were married in Hackney – in those days a pretty insalubrious place. I have had hopes of a Celtic strain somewhere, but they have faded. My mother and three aunts attended Oxford High School as I did, but gained no honours. There was nevertheless a certain tradition in the family of tough women and weak men. The spinster aunts went strong-mindedly into teaching, nursing, and the Civil Service, there being presumably a famine of young men after the slaughter of the Great War. My uncles were less forceful, perhaps taking after a jealous and pettish father. Uncle Ted went to the 'white man's grave' of the Gold Coast (Ghana), where he sickened of malaria and failed to return to a formidable wife; Uncle Charlie was ever so slightly scandalous: he left his wife, who later committed suicide, for the snares of a 'chorus girl'. They covered their shame by living in Canada. I met her there once; her kiss left an uncomfortably smeary mark on my cheek.

Clearly all the family made haste to leave the parental home except – as was customary for the youngest – my mother. But she was also by far the prettiest, and had turned away no end of 'proposals' before marrying at the late age of 24. Daughter and mother were always very close, with something of a love-hate tie, I think. She told me that Granny's fussing with her during labour must have been why she lost her first baby. But when the old lady was widowed and truly old, my mother would cycle up to Park Town nearly every day.

I wish I had learned more about Aunt Edith, now alive in my memory only for formidable false teeth and a car of the kind then appropriate for district nurses: it had to be started by winding a handle at the front, and the windows were made of a kind of orange celluloid. She had nursed at the front during the Great War and there had loved a doctor, but, my mother whispered, 'He was married'. She retired to Leamingon Spa, and didn't seem to me a romantic heroine; but how stupid I was not to have asked her about the life of a nurse in that war. She died of cancer like all the sisters.

Both Edith and Anne always came to us for Christmas at Rhodes House, and were given rainbow-striped gloves knitted by the cook from her scraps of wool. I wondered what they felt about their younger sister being now so grandly housed.

Upstairs in the Park Town house were two bedrooms with brass bedsteads; an interesting lavatory, and the 'sewing room.'

On the bedroom wall there was a print of Watts's 'Hope' that intrigued me. Crouching and blindfolded, barefooted in a chiffon dress, Hope sits on the globe and looks more like Despair. She is chained to something – perhaps a weaving frame? It's a powerful, rather sexy image, hung in many an old-fashioned room at the time, no doubt. I didn't know the pretty girl was Hope, so I sorrowed for her.

The sewing room next door was where I would be put down on the ottoman for my afternoon rest. This ottoman was of faded chintz and a long way from the Turkish empire; if you raised its lid there was to be found a Victorian pale pink silk dress, boned, frayed away at the creases. It had belonged to someone, I was told mysteriously, who had a 20-inch waist! Of course I didn't actually rest in the sewing room: I ransacked the boys' literature of uncles Ted and Charlie stacked there, and acquired early dreams of being a hero, running perhaps across the South African *veld* with news of the Boers, or dazzled by the Angel of Mons as I crouched in the trenches. There was a book, too, called *The Language of Flowers* that had a special fascination. I believed, somehow, that this was a code that I could learn, to communicate with... who? flowers? animals, like St Francis? nature? The sewing machine itself, a Singer now painted pink, I still have in my spare room. I made my children's clothes on it for some years.

The lavatory – one of only two for this family of eight plus servant – interested me because it had, instead of scratchy Bronco toilet paper, squares of newspaper pinned to the wall by a nail. And the toilet seat was a wide, built-in stretch of polished mahogany. When I moved in 1953 into my own first house, I think it was the similar Victorian mahogany bench that had drawn me. There was a great deal of mystique about this room. 'Do you want to pay a visit' or 'Have you done your duty today?', Granny would ask. If the answer was unsatisfactory, 'If at first you don't succeed, try, try, again' was the word. Toileting, obviously, was a question of agonising repression alternating with plucky facing up to duty.

It was on the top floor that the Park Town house became creepy. The bathroom! I never knew of it being used; it was a haunted place, icy cold, floored with cracked lino and echoing with the clank of distant rusty pipes. There was a gas geyser for heating water that would surely have exploded if it had ever been lit. Hot water, after all, was carried to bedrooms in jugs by the maid, chamber pots were under every bed. What need of a bathroom? Next to it were the maid's tiny room, and two empty bedrooms that smelled uncle-y, boyishly sweaty. Leather suitcases held shin pads and pairs of moth-eaten cricket whites.

Downstairs, last, to the kitchen, to me the most vivid still. It was everything the 'charmingly old-fashioned' kitchen of today shuns – small, dark, smelling of dishcloths. There were cupboards, something indistinct on the floor, an old range for firing with coal or wood that was no longer used in the 1930s. Instead there was some kind of gas stove in the scullery. Washing must have been done there too, for there was a short washing-line down the step. (In Garford Road, my mother had told me, washing-lines were forbidden: they might let down the neighbourhood.) A gate in the wall led out into a rustic lane that ran round the back of the gardens. When, some while ago, newspapers reported that a mother and baby were horribly attacked in a country lane, I saw it being here.

THE LONG VACATION

But the Park Town kitchen, like the Grannyish smell, had a certain sweetness. There was a table just the size for two to sit drinking mugs of tea. I often dream of kitchens, and in the Park Town one I am scrubbing and scrubbing at something dark and ancient and encrusted, This is not unpleasant, though – invigorating, rather.

What must the kitchenalia be nowadays at number 36? 'Units', certainly (that is, cupboards) not stainless steel – something rather expensively pine-y, in keeping with the age of the house. A freezer, a microwave, a washing machine. Something for tossing ingredients around. A toaster – no more toasting-forks in front of the sitting-room coal fire. A coffee grinder (coffee itself probably only known to an earlier Park Town in the form of bottled Camp Coffee, with its jolly label showing a sahib being brought a tray by black servant).

A rack for wine bottles. A garlic press. Steak knives, thermometer, omelette pan. Clingfilm, foil, laundry pegs of coloured plastic, not wood. Some of the old utensils, though, well scrubbed up, might have nostalgia value in an antique shop: the weighing machine, perhaps, with its set of polished brass weights so attractive to a child. From this kitchen emerged dishes certainly without sophistication but substantial enough to feed all eight if they were at home. Oh, and something for the maid, of course. And when I went for lunch with Granny, the kitchen produced lemon sago pudding, my favourite.

As for the bathroom what could it be now but *luxe, calme et volupté*? No spooks left there; all flushed away by the power shower. No rusty pipes, no freezing floor, no threatening geyser, no clanks and gurgles from far off.

THE LONG VACATION

A friend drove me on a memory trip recently round suburban Oxford, and we saw the current owner actually parking and going into the house. 'Go on, ring and ask him if you can look round,' she urged. But I couldn't. The house has to stay in my mind as it was, unchanged.

(ii)

Of course, throughout our childhoods my brother and I were still often at the Park Town house, taken by the current governess down South Parks Road and across the, University Parks, from which we emerged up a walled lane that echoed satisfactorily to our shouts. I don't believe the familiar mustiness in that house ever changed much; a telephone reluctantly installed in the 1930s was the only sign of modernity.

But how utterly different from gentle north Oxford was the home to which we moved when I was three years old. My father, by then Professor of Jurisprudence, was offered the job of Warden of Rhodes House, the centre for Rhodes Scholarships and embodiment of Cecil Rhodes' imperial dream. As an Australian who had left home just before the First World War and come to Oxford to study further, then fought throughout that war (two wounds, one medal), he was the man for the job. My mother, he often said, was at first seriously nervous at the prospect of running the Warden's Lodging – six indoor servants, the porter, the gardener, endless hospitality to be provided – but managed to do it superbly when the time came. So came about the huge change for our family. My parents' from their respectable but modest backgrounds, moved into the lifestyle of an aristocrat's stately home.

But first, one day after my brother was born, my father went off on a six-month tour of countries that were part of the Scholarship scheme. My mother was left with a baby and a three-year-old (me) and, for the moment, no particular home. Arrangements had fallen through; we went from pillar to post.

I added to my mother's vexations by upsetting a jug of boiling water over my arm at the Park Town house. There were screams and dramas, I'm told; my mother actually said later that there had been a question of amputating my arm, but this seems unlikely. 'You were angry about your baby brother', said a psychoanalyst some years later. Not at all. That hot water jug was very wobbly. I can see it, set out on the tea-tray, of rather pretty early Victorian silver, rounded above the base on a single foot: charming but highly unstable and just the thing to bring grief to a child in the care of an old lady. A crinkled scar is faintly visible on the arm beneath the wrinkles of old age. Only recently I had a dream where I fell down the steps of a plane and my arm fell off; I picked it up reluctantly and carried with me, knowing I mustn't abandon it.

* * * *

Cecil Rhodes had spent some six years in Africa when he wrote his *Confession of Faith*. His plan, he said, was for 'the bringing of the whole uncivilized world under British rule, for the recovery of the United States, for the making of the Anglo-Saxon race but one Empire.' For he believed, he said, 'that we are the finest race in the world, and that the more of the world we inhabit the better it is for the human race'. We may today be shocked, we may laugh indulgently; of course we don't use words like 'race' and 'uncivilized' any more, we don't dream, of empires – and, after all, the boy was only 23. But essentially, Rhodes' vision remained the same: ten years after the 'Confession' he was telling the House of Assembly in Cape Town that the 'barbarians of South Africa' must be treated like children and held under a system of despotism. Children, of course, who worked very hard and earned very little. The high-flying rhetoric, the cringe-making hubris may be put down to the assumptions of the age. But I know that historians who have studied the Rhodes record since have seen that the great imperial dream, as time went on, came to involve more and more cheating, lying, and greed. Power corrupted Rhodes; perhaps sometimes made him a little mad.

One worthwhile legacy, it is generally agreed, is the Rhodes Scholarship scheme that he set up in his Will. Fifty-two scholarships to Oxford University were to be awarded annually to students from the colonies, the United Sates, and Germany (a few only, added in a codicil after a visit to the Kaiser). The applicants were to be successful in 'manly sports' and to be outstanding for 'kindliness, unselfishness, manhood, and devotion to duty'. How they were to be assessed I don't know, but they sound lovely. A Committee was quickly set up after Rhodes' death, and got the scheme started. Its centre, Rhodes House, was not ready for another twenty-five years, however, so was 'born' a year later than myself. It was opened with a grand celebratory dinner attended by the Prince of Wales.

* * * *

This building stands imperiously in South Parks Road, opposite science laboratories from which I used to hear screams (monkeys? vivisection?).

In the 1920s the ground had been purchased from next-door Wadham College before it was quite certain what Rhodes House would be for. A statement, a monument to Empire? To Rhodes himself? A general meeting-place for the Scholars? A central library for colonial studies? Somewhere for a Warden to live and be able to entertain? It seems Milner, founding father, had wanted some sort of 'Cotswold manor house' – but died before he could put this forward. I like the sound of that rural manor, and think I would have preferred it as a home. Pevsner, in his 1974 review of Oxfordshire buildings, called the final edifice 'an oddity, but it has personality enough to rouse affection in some.' May we all be awarded such a judgement.

What the architect Sir Herbert Baker, creator of a Rhodes memorial on Table Mountain in South Africa, produced was an H-shaped building: a huge central hall, with to one side a library and rooms named after Rhodes's associates Beit and Jameson, and to the other side the Warden's Lodging, our house.

The public garden (no longer open to all) led on into our private garden, where sometimes tourists used to blunder in.

THE LONG VACATION

Rhodes House's special glory – or oddity? – is at its entrance: an echoing Rotunda, floored in marble (good for sliding on), Greek texts etched in gold around its high walls (I believe they said 'No Smoking'). A great, outdated celebration of empire! The Rotunda's dome is crowned outside by the 'Zimbabwe Bird' in bronze, copied from the famous ruins in the country once named after Rhodes, and formerly an emblem of British Africa. The same bird is carved in wood at the base of the main staircase in the house. I never had any idea what it was and, I think, never wondered. And the amazing Rotunda was just something that – like all children – I took for granted.

The cellars, where we were to shelter from Oxford's few bombs, were dark and creepy, but our home itself was luxurious. Some fifteen bedrooms with their own bathrooms (an unheard-of novelty then) imposing drawing-rooms and dining-room; a suite of offices; then behind the 'green baize door' (actually brown varnish) the kitchen quarters – scullery, pantry, larders, servants', sitting-room (where I once later tried to seduce a boyfriend), laundry-room, airing cupboards, and back stairs up to the maids' bedrooms. No en-suites there, though.

And the nursery quarters. Three bedrooms, two bathrooms, ironing room (where I once saved Rhodes House from burning down through an overheating iron), and the nursery itself, overlooking the Wadham Fellows' Garden where no one ever went. The nursery was rather far from the rest of the house; at meal times the kitchen had to be rung down on the internal telephone, a cook would send up the food on an internal lift, and it would be carried down the long corridor on a tray to the nursery. Quite far.

When I have dreams of Rhodes House now it is always under huge reconstruction: swimming pools are being dug, cellars excavated, rooms switched round or discovered; things sometimes tower, sometimes tunnel downwards, may shake precariously. Someone in the landscape, somewhere, may know what's going on. I thought these dreams were significantly special to me, but my brother, a very different character, has them too. They happen when life itself being shaken, is under reconstruction.

And indeed the house has undergone changes. Outside, the lawn in the public garden that was once a tennis court, then a wartime field of cabbages, is now a lawn again. The Static Water Tank built on another lawn as a defence against fire during an air-raid, has become a shrubbery. Inside... inside, I preferred it to stay as I remembered – but I did change my mind (see p. 188).

On the balcony that runs right round the top floor, possibly no one sunbathes naked now, unseen. And the huge portrait of Rhodes at the bottom of the staircase, leaning forward in the sunlight eager to grab some more of Africa? What's happened to that? Have they boldly left him there, or stacked him away in some dusty corner?

Family photographs now show me not in a suburban Oxford garden (sulking) but standing against noble stone walls (sulking). I now had an extra name, for the kitchen – *Miss* Rosemary. What had I left behind in Garford Road? Dear Jim, who loved me. A ginger cat called Marmalade, who 'had to go away because she had a canker in her ear', I was told. Poor Marmalade, no place for her in the new home. Perhaps a growing puzzlement about truth, and realness. And family life? Was that ever quite re-established, even after my father came back from what seemed a forever journey?

I don't remember anything as epic as a moving-in day – but there is a fragment from just before. An empty house, and I'm climbing many, many stairs with a little boy, not my infant brother but the head parlourmaid's nephew Leslie. The stairs were of fine polished wood and uncarpeted, and our footsteps echoed in a spacious emptiness bigger than I'd ever known. We did reach the top floor. It was brown lino up there, the nursery wing on one side and the servants' quarters on the other. In between, of course, a firmly closed door.

Once we had moved in, my brother and I lived up there with nannies. Our family's remove to an almost aristocratic setting didn't have that feature of the real aristocracy's home, the family nanny who stayed for life, nursing grandchildren in their turn. Our uniformed nannies came and went, some nicer than others. The first one, I believe, was rather nice, but she left to marry a farmer who told me the moon was made of green cheese. (Again, to believe these grown-ups or not?) Helen was a nice one. 'Why did Helen have to go?', I asked. 'Because she yawned while I was speaking to her', said my mother. Another puzzle.

The nursery was cosy, as nurseries should be. There was a spitting electric fire for toasting bread (where I once leaned too near and set my frizzy hair alight: such smell of singeing!), yellow walls and pale green painted furniture, a big dolls' house, a framed poster of *The Silent Pool*. (I believe this was a real place; where is it? I would like to track it down.) Later the nursery acquired a wind-up gramophone on which we played 'Butterflies in the Rain' and 'I'm Headin' for the Last Roundup'. It's odd how tunes and their words stay in mind longer than anything; I sometimes wake up with a tune in my head from some far, far off crevice of experience. Noel Coward noticed this ('extraordinary how potent cheap music is'); I don't think Proust mentions it. The gramophone had to have a tiny silver needle screwed into its head for each record. If it got too loud, socks were stuffed into the back of the mechanism.

The nanny's bedroom had a big, fenced-in balcony from which, once we had grown a few inches, my brother and I could look out over our wonderful garden, dominated by the Tree of Heaven (*Ailanthus altissima*). There was the enclosed kitchen garden where, when I was reading *The Rainbow*, I visualised the child Ursula leaving her shaming footmarks all over the seed beds: '*Why* were the footprints there? She had not wanted to make them. She stood dazzled with pain and shame and unreality.' I've always – not deliberately – seen fictional scenes as happening in familiar places. There are some that, even now, are firmly set in the house in Toronto where I lived for only three years.

There was the sandpit, the bicycle shed for jumping off the roof of, the rainwater butts humming with tiny flies, the greenhouse, the garage, the kitchen entrance. And the knife-sharpener. This was a kind of gritty mill-wheel standing in a base of water and turned by a handle. Knives would be held against the turning grit. I actually never saw it being done – though a blunt knife would not have been thrown away, any more than a sock with a hole in it. I last saw such a machine in the hands of a knife-grinder who used to call at my door here in London. I asked if I could buy it, but it was, he said, already promised to a museum.

The best of the garden was the high bank that ran right along the back, up to Wadham College's great copper beech (now horribly replaced by a conifer). It had been part of the city's defensive earthworks in the Civil War of the 1640's, I was told; Oxford of course was Royalist, so I was. Those cavaliers! The bank wasn't just a shrubbery: it was a place, a kind of complicated house of many rooms. The continuation of it beyond the fence next door was some other planet, savagely overgrown and weedy; I don't think I ever dared climb over there. The slope of our bank was covered in long grass, with daffodils in spring, and cut as hay in summer (for sliding down on), and topped by dense bushes that were excellent for games, hiding, and tête-à-têtes with little boys (Adrian had replaced Jim. He is now, I believe, a distinguished elderly cleric).

Here was my home, then, until I was sent to Canada in 1940 for fear of a German invasion. From here I walked to nearby Oxford High School – or preferably cycled, to avoid the flasher in Keble Road. From Rhodes House too I went down a path in the University Parks called Mesopotamia to swim in the teeth-chattering cold and muddy Dames' Delight – a fenced-off part of the river where once a dead sheep was stranded for days against the wire fencing.

Later I would often be sent off cycling to north Oxford to deliver notes to university homes, for tea on Sunday, perhaps, or sherry next week. Of course there was a Rhodes House porter for these errands, as well as the Royal Mail – but my mother was ferociously keen on fresh air and exercise for her children. My brother once attempted a revolt against these errands when he was in his teens, but without success. He now detests the bicycle.

My very first bicycle was of course at Rhodes House. It was called a Fairy Cycle and had little stabilizers on the back wheel for absolute beginners. I see it in my mind's eye as being tried out on my fifth birthday just outside the bike shed. The stabilisers would be pushed back, and you ventured along with a grown-up hand guiding from the back. One day the hand would be stealthily withdrawn and you flew free. Independent locomotion! A great step in life, cycling up and down the pavement of South Parks Road. Passers-by smiled indulgently. Even better was roller-skating the same stretch later on, on clunky skates with leather straps; or, when polish was being laid down in the Milner Hall, being dragged up and down the boards on a blanket, a human polishing machine, shrieking with laughter.

There are these and other happy memories of the Rhodes House years. Looking out of my bedroom window to hear music and see Japanese lanterns hung around the dark garden when there was a party downstairs. Riding my bicycle round and round the lawn while I tried to stand up on the saddle, as I'd just seen done at the circus. Being brought out of the Cathedral where I'd been reading the Table of Affinities in the Prayer Book, before Dean

Lowe's boring sermon, and out into Tom Quad quite empty in the sunlight, to look at goldfish in the pond and the Mercury statue poised above them. Lying under a special chestnut tree on the Rhodes House bank and staring up into the leaves – the best of all for staring into – with our black cat up on the wall watching the traffic of South Parks Road.

Beyond, there was the covered market, where I was often steered by shopping nannies. It seemed then a kind of centre of the whole city. All the basics could be bought there – meat, fruit and veg, bread and cakes – but for my brother and me the best of the market was the pet shop. There was no law then against the putting of puppies and kittens in the shop window: we would squeeze up against the glass and tap for the hopeful little creatures inside.

There was only one external phone in Rhodes House, standing in the hall on a mahogany table. For guests wanting to pay for calls there was a money-box labelled 'Kingsley Fairbridge Farm Schools'. These Farm Schools were founded by a white South African who, visiting London in 1903, was appalled by the poverty he saw. To sweep the children of the slums into imperial, open spaces seemed, surely, a practical idea?

> I saw great Colleges of Agriculture springing up in every man-hungry corner of the Empire. I saw children shedding the bondage of bitter circumstances and stretching their legs and minds amid the thousand interests of the farm. I saw waste turned into providence, the waste of un-needed humanity converted to the husbandry of unpeopled acres.

THE LONG VACATION

Fairbridge won a Rhodes Scholarship in 1908, and he died young, leaving a respected reputation as founder of child migration schemes. Nowadays, dumping children like sacks of cargo in a remote new country seems abominable. But have we ever seen anything like the slums Fairbridge encountered at the turn of the last century – children in rags, without shoes, underfed and dying from infections or stacked into orphanages?[1]

Down in the Rhodes House cellars there were exciting trunks – the 'dressing-up boxes' – filled with clothes from the days of my parents' amateur dramatics. Milkmaidy clothes – frilled aprons and floppy bonnets – pageboy tights, and an orange jerkin cut out by some rather unsteady scissors; red gipsy skirts with wool embroidery round the hem; a 19th century satin bodice with an unbelievably tiny waist. My friend Catherine and I draped ourselves in these things and wandered about the house irritating the servants and the secretaries. My mother made some attempts to enrol me into amateur stage performances – wasn't there a sailor costume, and a hornpipe dance? – but I was terrified, and always managed to run a sore throat to avoid them.

---

[1] Not all migrant children were well treated. I had an astonishing letter some years ago from Nova Scotia: 'We think we may have the same grandparents as you'. Marilyn Verge was the daughter of a man who had been sent out to a farm as a young child; my Uncle Ted's wife, it seemed, had had an 'illegitimate' baby for a few years before she had to send him off. What else could she do? He had had a hard life out there and was now very old. I was able to send him his mother's prayer-book and am told he kept it always beside him.

THE LONG VACATION

If not dressing up or making fudge with Catherine at the St John's College lodgings (later on, poring over diagrams of the womb), I might be visiting Griselda, who lived in a Christ Church lodging overlooking the Tom Quad because her father was Dean of Oxford Cathedral. Behind, there was a college garden; we roamed underneath the huge mulberry tree while she explained to me churchy things like plainsong and enclosed nuns. At that time I had lost belief in a literal Christianity – though there was certainly some fearful Judge watching my every thought. The nuns from St Frideswide's near to Rhodes House frightened me in their sweeping black clothes, even though they smiled kindly at children. Griselda's family, in spite of the high clerical status, were somewhat disapproved of at home because there were no less than *four* children. Which was perhaps slovenly, even a little common. Two children, at that time, was the thing for decent parents.

I'm glad I did have a Bible education. Although in my teens I opted out of the Cathedral services on grounds of headache, toothache and such like (in this family things were never to be declared frankly) and never then entered a church except on a foreign sightseeing footing, now I am old I do like to revisit Christianity's two millennia of art, music, poetry, and stories – what Iris Murdoch has called 'refuges, lights, visions, deep sources, protections, strongholds, foothold, icons, starting points, sacraments, pearls of great price'. Now the Christian story has run its course, biblical research making it impossible to take literally and our stupid minds impossible to enjoy mythically. Murdoch did try so hard to connect these pearls of great price with real moral dilemmas, and after death appeared in a dream of mine asking urgently, 'Where's the key? I've lost the key.'

When, out in Toronto, I had passed some exam or other, my father sent a cablegram (a rare transatlantic thing): 'Many daughters have done virtuously, but thou hast excelled them all.' From his pious upbringing he knew his Bible, though he came to hate Christianity.

Around this time, the wondrously eccentric Pitt-Rivers Museum in Oxford might become a source of entertainment for us. Special lectures for children were laid on, one of which – a very pungent one on chemistry – caused me to be sick down the whole length of a fine stone staircase. I felt, I remember, a certain pride. But the real highlight of the year, our annual St Giles' Fair, was in summer. The early thrill was seeing the big vans arriving to park in Keble Road, all through the day before. Then on the first day itself, faint music from steam organs could be heard if the wind blew the right way – and joy would be about to begin. At one end, up by the War Memorial at the junction of the Woodstock and Banbury Road, stood the scary helter-skelter, a twirling slide-down kind of lighthouse. Two mighty, gaudy steam roundabouts were kings of the fair costing as much as sixpence a ride – similar ones painted and reconditioned, come to a fair opposite my house in London now and there is no finer ride than on a dragon or a horse, with a grandchild on lap. The stall with pink candyfloss that shrank to a nugget on the tongue, and the cream-filled brandysnaps, was up by the Martyrs' Memorial. The Big Wheel, on which my mother as a child was stranded at the top when something got stuck, creakingly wheeled and wheeled. Nearby was the coconut shy, where I won a coconut that resisted all attempts to crack it open.

The centre (for me) of the Fair was very frightening indeed. A billboard above the Headless Lady's tent showed her sitting on a chair, her body ending at the neck. From the stump a tube rose up and drooped into a jar! It was very haunting. Children had seen no horror films then; I was not to be allowed to go inside and see her until I was twelve. And when I did reach twelve, in 1940, I was evacuated away from an expected invasion to Canada, a month before the Fair arrived. When I came back to England at fifteen years old, the Fair was still circulating; but the Headless Lady and her tent had gone.

It seems obvious how she could have been faked up – and yet at eleven I think I believed that there was something real and horrible in there. I suspect I went on believing in a whole lot of strangenesses for a long time. And hadn't I read about the guillotine *tricoteuses* with their baskets of heads? And been wheeled, resisting into an operating theatre? (If I stopped screaming, they said, my Mummy would be in the 'theatre'. She wasn't).

* * * *

That particular memory is a vivid and bodily one, still humming somewhere in the coils of my brain. The strongest memories are these shivery slippery ones: smells, tastes, textures; glimpses and sudden startles. The scent of my mother's powder puff, kept in a silver-topped bowl;

the coolness of my embroidered white dress made (I was told) from linen intended for some foreign Queen's sheets; the wiry prickle of a flower circlet on the brow: all of them madeleines. The circlet of buttercups was part of a bridesmaid's outfit. We were dressed, myself and some other child, in the Park Town front bedroom in pale green shantung tunics with petal-shaped hems – very 1930s, very faerie and woodsy, more charming, I think, than today's white frills and fuss. It was the time when girl babies were being christened, in fresh-air fashion, Heather and Hazel and Joy and April and June – and, of course, Rosemary. If only my parents had stuck to their other choice, Clemency – but there's always the name dropped for a safer one. My sons just escaped being Merlin or Bruno or Bartholomew or Tobias. Or, from an earlier choice, when I lay still awake after Ovaltine on a summer evening, Lancelot, Gawain, Pelleas and Mordred, with sisters Ruby, Pearl, Emerald and Diamond.

These plans must have alternated with cabin-boy ones. And – now a sudden memory, with a picture of a white horse that would be my own to go about on and hitch up to a post when I got off. The swaggering feel of it! And best of such pictures, a little hut in a forest all to myself, arranged and furnished and cooked in by myself. Grown up, I bought a ramshackle cottage on the Welsh border. Though I sold it twenty years ago as I began to get old, it hasn't ceased to run through my (sleeping) dreams. Sometimes I'm looking at holes in the roof, sometimes planning to shore up an extra room. It's always vivid and yet unsatisfactory, because it's a reflection of constructing a life. Judging by the magazines, the 'buying a wreck and transforming it' motif is a deeply cherished fantasy at the present time.

* * * *

It's a great bonus to be able to produce eccentric uncles, but my maternal ones were in Africa and Canada and the other four in Australia. There was uncle Eric, of course (a godfather), a sweet and aged Bertie Wooster who used words like 'old bean', and 'boodle'. The old bean did have a lot of boodle, and left me a diamond brooch that I sold to pay the psychoanalyst. But the best I can produce is Uncle Fred. He too was *rich* rich, had two houses and a boat. In Rhodes House my parents were hardly strapped for cash – there were surely huge expenses allowed for hospitality and for a large staff – but Uncle Fred was rich. The fortune was presumably made in the early days of the South African mines, by what we now have to call slave labour. He had been, I was told, in the Jameson Raid, which meant nothing to me at the time except that one of the Rhodes House halls was called the Jameson Room. It is odd to think that the gruff old man that I knew was involved in that wild adventure. I never even heard him mention Rhodes. The raid against the Boers led by Jameson was nearly disastrous for Rhodes; 'Twenty years we have been friends, and now he goes and ruins me!', he groaned.

Later in my suspicious teens, I wondered if Uncle Fred wasn't something of a crook. He had the looks and manner for it: a bristly red nose that I associate with the word 'grog' (but I've no reason to think he was an alcoholic), and a growl of a voice suggesting decades of expensive cigars. I once heard that voice, some time after the war, drop the remark that 'What this country needs is more unemployment!' 'Now, now, Fred', said my father.

I think now that he was no crook, unless by acquiring a South African fortune. He was certainly hugely gregarious and generous, and I have an idea that on the Hellenic cruise of 1937, for instance, he paid for the whole group of friends that he took. He gave my mother much jewellery (from South African mines?), some of which I inherited until a window cleaner stole it all. As well as the christening Bible from him that I am glad to keep, I still have a pair of emerald earrings, but they are too uncomfortable to wear.

I just felt, as a child, that silly old Uncle Fred's household was always drawing Mummy and Daddy away for holidays. We two children did once, with the nanny, stay at his Devon holiday house and had milk in cardboard cartons rather than bottles, which was exciting. But I have an overshadowing feeling, as so often, that I was in some way especially disapproved of there. There was some little girl nearby who was much, much less troublesome.

* * * *

On their long tour of South Africa, when my brother and I were aged two and five, we had been sent to a Home in Kent for children without parents for five months. A new nanny, it seems, had failed to turn up. This place I only visit in my dreams, when I am in a narrow cubicled room, or being hustled into an enormous bath with a crowd of other children. There was a chestnut tree, and underneath it a bee caught, buzzing, in my frizzy hair. A stronger memory of these months is of a beach of very pale, dry sand with spiky leaves pushing through it. Aunt Anne was there and her friend. There was a happy feeling then: Anne was the best of aunts (though, sadly for her, the plainest) and I suspect she drew me back from the separation gulf by taking us out for a day from the Home. My two-year-old brother, though, lost his very identity down there: he went into the Home as Christopher and emerged as Kit. There was another child with the same name. He remembers nothing of it, but has a dream in which he looks into a mirror and sees no one there.

I was still clinging on to fairies and magic there – a counterweight to my struggle over finding out the truth of things. Religion dwindled; the Cathedral service, the gloriously glowing windows – cursing of the fig tree I liked, against such a blue glass sky – would be followed by dull Sunday School at St Aldates', instituted by a particularly nasty governess who I knew had her eye on the curate. At home, sins like cycling on the grass might be followed by punishment.

Punishment. The bell tolls. My grandchildren maybe little savages, but at least they hardly, I think, know what the word means. For my generation it was taken for granted in the rearing of children; but I don't know if it was as obliterating for all as it was for me – and of course I may have especially deserved it. Punishment was not just a

THE LONG VACATION

withdrawal of pocket-money or privilege, but of all proof of existence. On punishment days my mother, who normally would come up to the nursery wing at bedtime for lullabies and story-reading, ceased to speak or look at me – not just for hours but sometimes for as long as days. This practice was continued for all of her lifetime; I remember well how it felt at mealtimes, when I was an adult. (Indeed, my typing gets into a strange muddle as I try to get these words down). Between the bright, almost unnaturally bright, mother and the absolutely silent one was a black gulf into which I fell, only seeing a ray of dawn when I might be asked, in a rather specially high voice, to pass the butter. Separation and punishment became inextricably linked, for ever after.

It followed on, I suppose, from the sullenly silent grandfather my aunt told me about. There was also – and I can hardly believe my own clear memory here – there might be talk of the 'reformatory'. I suppose this was an early term for some kind of Borstal – but it was used in all seriousness. I remember too a conversation that began with, 'The Catholic priests say that by the time a child is seven its character is set' and went on to doubt whether I still had time to reform. (The crimes in question, incidentally, were variations of disobedience. In particular, arguing.) It was suggested more than once that I repeat to myself, 'Day by day, in every way, I am getting better and better'[2]. Whether I carried this out or not I don't know – I

---

[2] This must have been some memory of Emile Coué's 'autosuggestion' of the early 20th century. Repeating this mantra was supposed to work wonders. I still intend to try it.

only remember most earnestly writing out a list of my 'Resolutions'. They didn't work.

Sad, those Resolutions. That they presumably never worked, and that they had to be made at all.

The reformatory-style conversations were never carried out in my father's presence. I realise that up to this point in my account he has been upstaged by my mother (though when they met through amateur dramatics, he was playing the larger roles). Why is it so difficult to bring him into the picture, when I was more deeply 'fond' of him than of my mother (whatever that so English-y word means)? The energy that has pushed my mother forward in my story is, I fear, partly hurt and resentment. And I had so wanted to gloss them over. Underneath them, I know, was a desperate dependence. With my father things were less complicated. Were they? I think so. I looked up to him; he called me 'honeybun'; he didn't do reformatory talk, though he was a strict man.

Growing up in Australia and, like my mother, the youngest of six children; he was the son of a distinguished cleric in the Congregational Church, which a century ago was a rather bold and forward-looking nonconformist body. A photograph of this grandfather's tombstone shows the engraving: 'Well done, thou good and faithful servant. Enter into the joy of thy Lord'. My father told us very little about Australian life: that there were sharks, that he had fallen asleep in the sun once and had to go to hospital with burns, that he had faced an enormous snake. Australian presents used to arrive from the unknown grandparents – a fur muff in the form of a koala bear, a book about kookaburras and gum trees – so I had a rough idea of Australia, though no passionate interest in it.

It was a clever family, for the boys, at any rate; the two sisters of course became housewives. One brother rose to become head of an Australian college, another published slim volumes of poetry. It was also a poor one (I believe I was told that the annual stipend was £90) and very, very pious. Family prayers, no alcohol, no Sunday entertainment, no dancing, no playgoing. This grandfather, the story goes, was himself the son of a tough and successful immigrant, and before he saw the light and went into the Church, he started life as a travelling actor. This I think is fact and no family myth: my father inherited the acting gene, and played no mean Julius Caesar with the Oxford University Dramatic Society in 1913.

That intense family piety, and his experiences in the Great War, made him, however, a strong enemy of religion. *He* certainly did not come with us to Oxford Cathedral on a Sunday morning. It was odd, even though I was grown up at the time, to hear my serious and conventional father once say that such-and-such (baptism? tithes? Sunday School?) was 'one of the Church's worst rackets'.

Through scholarships he made his way to university in Australia and then in 1909 to Oxford to read law. A few faint snapshots survive from that pre-war time. Strange! He looks just like any undergraduate, apart from the moustache: relaxed, laughing with friends, smoking of course. He smoked and smoked, always Gold Flake. It would have been odd, at that time, for a man not to smoke. He was to become so much more stiff, even grave, in old

THE LONG VACATION

age; rather grim (was it our fault, his children's? We felt it might be.) By the time of the Rhodes House years there was certainly no question of pious poverty.

He joined the army, I understand, at the start of the First World War and stayed on to the end, apart from some hospital leave. Two medals. I have some very, very faded letters from the Front, and I can just decipher this passage from a letter to his brother:

> At dusk set out on horseback with a mounted orderly and duly arrived at the place indicated. It was an elaborately constructed dug-out with a complete set of rooms underground. I waited there for a couple of hours. After I had been there some time, a Brigadier came in with his Brigadier Major and Staff Captain. He, too, was awaiting news; and when at last it came, it was bad news. The 'stunt' had failed completely. I felt a sort of melancholy interest in observing the directors of operations at their councils. The General and his staff took the news very much as any of us subalterns would take it, with mingled disappointment, resignation, and perplexity. And I imagine that is how bad news comes to General Head Quarters too. Studious and elaborate preparation – some detail goes wrong – 'It's a wash-out, Reggie: start again.' After all, no other comment is possible.

'On horse among the falling shells', he writes later. This led on to a gas attack: my failing eyesight gives out here, over the faint, flimsy page. Some died, I think; my father escaped with a bad headache.

My brother and I, as in so many families, were not told anything about these experiences in that horrible war; it was, I imagine, beyond recounting. And yet, as an adult, I heard him say, 'I wouldn't have missed it for the world' – and was amazed, because I knew about its horrors by then. And in a letter from post-war Oxford to his brother in Australia, I find him saying that he feels lost without his army life. He never revisited Australia apart from a home leave in 1916. As for Rhodes's mission and the glory of imperialism, I never heard him say anything about that.

* * * *

I was, though, quite aware of a different aspect of grown-up life: *class*. Of 'us' and 'them'. The 'them' were not just the actually poor but the not-quite-us, who were often encountered. They were identified by a slight mispronunciation of vowels. There were the servants, of course, with the rural Oxfordshire accent, who had to call me Miss Rosemary, while I scarcely knew their second names. (They had first names that have now become very fashionable but were then kitchen names – Emma, Lily, Amy, Kate.) They were obviously Them and yet lived under our roof and could be rather firm. My brother and I were not encouraged to go into the kitchen or scullery, and certainly not into the windy larder, where huge joints and puddings were stacked under domes of wire mesh. (These were, of course, pre-war joints and puddings.) Our cook at that time was a stone-deaf village woman who could

THE LONG VACATION

hardly articulate. And yet she must somehow have been taught to read, for my mother went out to the kitchen each day and wrote the day's menu on a slate. When I came back from evacuation in Canada, Emma was gone. She had been run over by a car in the blackout – unable, of course, to hear it coming.

There were two working-class homes that we sometimes went into. One was Mrs and Miss Richards' house, a mean terraced villa by the canal. As an undergraduate my father had lodged with them for a time, and it seemed they had never forgotten it: we were greeted with shouts of welcome and excitement when we visited. Amy Richards was a huge-breasted lady, her mother wizened and tiny; at some time there must have been a Mr Richards, but I never heard anything about him. In their sitting-room there was a large framed photograph of myself simpering on one papered wall (wallpaper was rather working-class and all the servants at Rhodes House had it in their bedrooms), and one of my brother, clutching his toy monkey, on the other. I would usually be sent out the back to 'play' with a grandchild. 'Do you do phonetics at your school?', I asked, 'No', she said. We looked thoughtfully at the oily canal.

After we left, my father would always remark how odd it was that sometimes you do a lot for someone and get no thanks, but sometimes you do nothing very much and get heaped with praise and affection.

A cramped piece of Victoriana like the Richards' (not unlike the rather valuable Victorian hovel I now live in) would be entirely clean; but it smelt differently from home. The big spaces of Rhodes House had no smell, windows were open, chilly garden breezes blew through. Even the lofty kitchen retained little smell of actual cooking. What the Richards' house smelled of – unobtrusively – was sour dishcloths hung out to dry.

Another home we went into belonged to Miss Fathers the dressmaker. Down Plantation Road, past the baker's where we liked to watch shelves of loaves being brought out of the oven, she lived up a flight of steps with her sewing-machine. The same smell, rather stronger. Miss Fathers was very stout, dressed in heavy black, and had a goitre under her chin. She would run up, I suppose, little pairs of pyjamas and the like. Her window looked out on something grey and ashy.

These were the few glimpses I had of how ordinary people lived, and I was far from oblivious of how different this was from my home. The butcher, who sent round meat by a boy with a capacious bicycle basket, would be working-class (though I had never, ever, heard this word). The boy on the bike? The errand-boy, a lad who had left school at the usual age of fourteen and whistled as he rode. Errand-boys were known to whistle a lot, and liked to live up to their reputation. The coal man, covered in black dust and heaving a huge sack of nutty slack down the coal-hole to feed Rhodes House's basement furnaces, was clearly not-us: even the old shire horses that pulled his lorry looked dusted-over and wretched. At the bottom of the scale were *tramps:* the actually ragged, who called at the kitchen door for scraps. We were told to stay clear of them.

As for anyone with a naturally dark skin, not blackened by coal dust, I never saw such a person except in a geography textbook. Gandhi, I understand, visited Rhodes House some time in the '30s, but I never saw him. I know

THE LONG VACATION

of the great man's visit because it was such a source of comedy to my mother; he wore a dhoti! And had an 'accent'! Accents were a huge source of interest and amusement then (and presumably of anxiety[3]). 'Haow naow braown caow' (supposedly a lower-class sound) would raise a merry laugh. Similarly, nearer the war, when German academics were fleeing to Oxford from Nazi Germany, their accent could raise a smile. 'One of the race of Israel, I think', I heard my father murmur with a grin.

I don't want to accuse my parents of being exceptionally racist or snobbish. No, it was all just the normal and horrible snobbery of the time, worse than can be imagined today. The Them, the not-one-of-us, were not unfortunate, not threatening revolution, but so *comical*, you see. Look through popular novels of the time and you will find many a comical charwoman or gardener. Marie Antoinette, when she said, 'Let them eat cake', was perhaps just trying to raise a good laugh.

And yet, when there was a local election just before the war, I proudly wore a blue rosette on my gym tunic, for Quentin Hogg (later Lord Hailsham). Of course! My parents were Conservative: wasn't everyone? I hadn't yet the ability to connect my unease about Miss Fathers' workroom with the colour of my rosette. The breakthrough came only later, when I was a schoolgirl in Canada. Our teacher set us a political debate between Left and Right; we were arbitrarily assigned to one or the other

---

[3] J. B. Priestley from the provinces has recorded how on coming south he had to subdue his accent: there was no option. (How did Lawrence's voice mutate, I wonder?) Scottish and Southern Irish, however, were acceptably quaint.

side, and I was given Left. To bone up on the background, I got Shaw's *Intelligent Women's Guide to Socialism and Capitalism* from the school library – and never looked back His arguments were so clear, the conclusions so obvious. I wrote across the Atlantic to my parents, half joking, half anxious: 'I hope you're not bloated capitalists!'. My father wrote back that they were capitalists, but not bloated ones.

I wish I had those transatlantic letters now: they would restore so much of what is numbly forgotten. My mother threw them away, along with my undergraduate essays, when I was away working in Paris rather than helping her move house.

I re-read the Shaw quite recently, out of curiosity It is astonishingly boring. But the arguments, the conclusions, for me still march on[4]. That was one of the few things I gained from Canadian school, I think: that, and a visit to a soap factory. The huge vats, the unforgettable smell. The idea of ever, ever having to work there.

* * * *

Meanwhile, downstairs from the Oxford nursery, life was going on as before: voices from formal dinner parties heard over the banisters, boring grown-up visitors always coming and going, fusses about servants, and parents away again with Uncle Fred or on Rhodes business. Upstairs in the nursery, the nearest I got to South African

---

[4] I know, goalposts have moved; I trip over goalposts all the time. Yet I still could never vote Rightwards.

exploits was in books, without knowing it. Henty, Rider Haggard, John Buchan, Conan Doyle, Anthony Hope, and my uncles' 1890ish boys' magazines at Park Town; wasn't there a whiff of the open *veld* there, of wild early days? I was hooked on adventure. Even ironing my Girl Guide tie and polishing my badge took me a step nearer to it, Didn't the very words 'scout' and 'guide' date from South African days? And the badges for tracking and making camp fires without matches? It was that adventure-lust that led me to make the mistake of agreeing in 1940 to go with the Canadian evacuation scheme. Red Indians, I thought. Beavers. Trackless wilderness.

There was a living author I much admired at the time. He called himself 'Grey Owl', though I believe he was unmasked as Archibald Delaney, a Canadian. He wore his hair in a coal-black pigtail and dressed in the costume. I had his books about wilderness lore, and when he came to lecture at the Town Hall I was a ten-year-old groupie. And there was an exciting 'Gypsy Petulengro' who wrote in Arthur Mee's *Children's Newspaper*, an otherwise sober and colourless publication. Is that why I belong to the Gypsy Council now, and follow Roma news with interest? From a car window, gypsies could sometimes be seen then round a campfire by the roadside. I tried to learn some Romany. (People are starting to use the word 'chav' as one of the many terms for a low sort of person; they should know that a 'Romani chav' just means a 'gypsy fellow.')

Adventure might mean running off to be a gypsy or a cabin boy. There was a book called *Rocked in the Cradle of the Deep* that was dear to me. And Robert Louis Stevenson, of course. I had the luck to be re-reading *Kidnapped* thirty years later aboard a small sailing boat just as we passed the very place where David Balfour would have been running across the wild moorland.

After finishing a book (and I remember *panic* on seeing that there was only half an inch of pages of *The Three Musketeers* left) I was for a while one of the characters in it. I walked that way, gazed out of windows that way, smiled whimsically that way. My moment-to-moment thoughts were all phrased in 'she' mode. 'She walked downstairs, gazed out of the window and smiled whimsically.' (I had some difficulty with 'her eyes twinkled'.) 'She put on her gym tunic. It was too long.' 'Slowly she finished the last page, and bowed her head.' It meant that the *she* was watched, was part of a story, was not alone in a gap. And that I had sucked something out of an author's imagination and brought it right into my bones. After I saw my first *Hamlet* – John Gielgud's – I walked with his specially elegant, slightly dragging step for days. I am still inclined to pretend, 'sense', or whatever the word is, that I am *watched*.

* * * *

My parents' friend John Masefield, now forgotten but then Poet Laureate, took a shine to me around this time – I must have talked of cabin boys and full-rigged sailing ships – and began to send me little packages of photos and drawings of these vessels. I would stick them into an album. But at ten years old interests change fast: I was moving on to *Malory and the Knights of the Round Table*. My ambition to learn the full rigging of ships off by heart was foundering like a boat in a tropical storm. Yet I have only *today* discovered a tiny remnant of the many pictures he sent: a yellowed newspaper cutting of a fine four-master with at least twenty billowing sails. Perhaps these pictures did feed into my later passion for sailing on small boats. The kindly poet also inscribed some of his books to me, sketching in a tiny watercolour of myself ballet-dancing, for this was another passion. I don't think I read the poet's works then, except for his lovely children's stories; if I had read his narrative poem *Dauber*, heartbreakingly based on his own time before the mast, I would surely have abandoned cabin-boy ambitions. I hope Masefield is some day rescued from oblivion. His *In the Mill* is a gentle, astonishing record of being penniless and adrift in the United States – a far cry from the fine house he had later at Boar's Hill outside Oxford.

There was theatre for us too. A matinée of the splendid and patriotic *Where the Rainbow Ends*, a story of our patron saint (no longer politically correct) conquering a foe. After seeing it I wore a St George badge on my gym tunic, next to my Ovaltineys badge. (Ovaltineys, of course, had a slot on Radio Luxembourg on Sundays – a shrewd marketing move by the makers of that disgusting drink. Our enemies were the Cococubs.) There was a production of *The Tempest* – my first Shakespeare, I think – which entranced me. It was put on by the boys of the Dragon School (which took boys only, up to the age of about thirteen): so I realise now that what entranced me was all played *by little boys!*

And the pantomime, at what was then the New Theatre! Such laughs – though sometimes I didn't quite understand the jokes. We sang about a blacksmith: 'Underneath the spreading chestnut tree, I loved her and she loved me,' we piped. 'Now you ought to see our fam-il-ee'... and so on. Penny whistles had been passed along the rows, and we blew along gloriously to the tune.

I especially liked 'Every little girl would like to be / The fairy on the Christmas tree...'. Christmas was so hugely stoked up with promises. On Christmas Day you couldn't really get punished for anything. Some weeks before, we would have been called down to the kitchen to stir the Christmas pudding mix and make a wish. When a 5p piece fell out of my handbag the other day. I suddenly felt again that special moment when, on the day itself, the spoon turned up a farthing in the pudding. There was no fussiness about wrapping the hidden treasures up in paper, and the Christmas tree was lit by wobbly candles – horribly dangerous as it now seems.

When I was told that Father Christmas wasn't real, I understand I was enraged and amazed. Nowadays, like many people, I am rather depressed over the Christmas season. It's partly the weeks of jingle and hype in the shops: this wasn't so crushingly jolly in earlier days. Or are we perhaps all disappointed that Father Christmas isn't real? That no one's watching out for us, that nothing we long for arrives overnight, that magic itself wilts under scrutiny?

THE LONG VACATION

* * *

Yet I can still smell that stirred pudding mix. Even the pages of books had strange and different smells then. Some – I don't know why – smelt sad or ominous and made me want to cry. To try to track these down I have sniffed my few remaining nursery books, rejected by grandchildren. *The Wind in the Willows*? Nothing. *Uncle Remus*? Nothing. *The Ameliorator* by E. V. Lucas.

Still nothing. Pages need to be fresher, more inky, perhaps? Kingsley's *The Heroes,* if I plunge my nose against its browned pages, does faintly smell, though it seems at first just a scent of age and mustiness. But when I go through the chapter, 'How Perseus Slew the Gorgon' – how he walked across the Ister dry-shod to the Unshapen Land to find the three Grey Sisters, who had but one eye and one tooth between them, 'beneath the cold white winter moon, where neither seal nor sea-gull dare come near, lest the ice should crush them in its claws' – then with the book-smell I get a whiff of the awe and frozen fear this once held. I still can reach it, thank goodness.

Smells of illness; a different range of fear. Real illness, in the London Clinic, was itself the Unshapen Land that has no name. Blood-on-bandage smell. And the pervasive antiseptic: unscrewing a bottle of Dettol is a miniature desolation, like the chloroform smell from a bottle of nail-polish remover. But the little illnesses were dealt with very sweetly: a flickering night-light, a jug of Friar's Balsam to inhale, a sense of late-night specialness. If ill, one was out of the reach of naughtiness and punishment. By day, Vicks Vapour Rub would be massaged into the small bony chest, a piece of flannel spread across and pinned to the Liberty bodice, and from the mix of the warmth and the Vick's, an eye-watering wave of smell would float up. (Proust, perhaps, had this treatment for his childhood asthma – something much more brutally reminiscent than the delicate madeleine.)

Sensations, sensations. The crackle of my frizzy hair being brushed by a Mason Pearson brush and giving out sparks. The horrible taste of sweet-sounding laxative Syrup of Figs, the chalky one of Milk of Magnesia, the faint one of Parish's Chemical Food, said to be a source of iron, and taken through a straw lest it turn teeth *black*. The satin feel on my arms of a cloak made for me, blue velvet lined with a golden colour (the High School colours) and the silver party slippers to go with it that were of course carried in a shoe-bag, the one with my initials embroidered on it in wonky cross-stitch by myself. A flicker of light still comes down from the silver slippers, and – suddenly – from the huge silver salver down in the front hall, put out for calling cards. 'Calling' was a ritual: those who, mistakenly or deliberately , called at the wrong time – during an afternoon nap, perhaps – left a card to show that they *had been*. The having been there was the point, a kind of metaphysical one. Above the silver platter, high on the wall, hung the huge hairy head of some uncouth South African beast.

* * * *

Pleasures. Sensations. Flickerings and gleams. But always those partings. It was a long time before I realised that this was not the case in other university families, for children of professors or heads of colleges, for instance. During these absences the gap, the black gulf became frighteningly near. Chaos seemed possible. Cooks and housemaids giggled on the back stairs. The porter, horrifyingly, came in and sipped tea in the kitchen itself.

One of the kinder nannies thought out a scheme for me: we cut out a paper spider with – let's say – forty legs, and every day pulled off a leg and got nearer to the day when they would come back, and bring the light.

Once I tried to invent a scheme for myself. I wanted to be able to *find* something after they'd gone, to discover, to be surprised, to be brought to life. I asked my mother if she could arrange a present for me to be hidden so that I could find it when they were gone. Ingenious for an eight-year-old? But now there was a much less nice nanny, who just put it on my bed once they had left. There was no discovery, no seeking and finding and *conquering* the absence. I can see that picture: it was called something like *The Fairy Piper* and showed a gobliny sort of man piping to a galaxy of wondrously transparent fairies – you could see through them! I still hadn't got fairies out of my system, though I was embarrassed about them. On some special night – St John's Eve, I think – one should definitely be able to see them – I couldn't; but it must have been because I wasn't the seventh child of a seventh child. Families just weren't big enough.

So, parents went off to Devon and Cornwall, Portmeirion in Wales, the Lake District, Norfolk; on Hellenic Greek cruises; to the French Riviera. I still see the deep, deep blue of the sky painted on those primitive postcards from France. I have vases, paintings, strings of beads in that colour and, just occasionally, it appears in a dream, signalling a sweetness. And of course there were long Rhodes Trust journeys to South Africa and the United States. (Never, though, to Australia. Clearly my father had no great wish to revisit it, though some Australian relatives came over to stay with us.)

Almost unawares, separation became a lifetime's preoccupation.

From all I know of my parents' childhoods, they had none of these partings – their parents were ordinary enough not to dream of going away on their own. The idea of 'recharging batteries', recovering from a 'hectic' term, might have puzzled them. I have always thought this must be why my parents went through life with so much more confidence than my brother and myself. ('We weren't always confident; we just worked hard,' I hear them arguing back. It is a terrible thing to accuse those who are beyond arguing.)

I had a slightly guilty knowledge that I didn't want to look at. It was that Mummy was a cheat – three times over. The first was when I was brought down to read to a visitor. 'She can read already!' But I had the passage by heart, and she knew I did: it wasn't reading. The second time concerned a children's colouring competition. In the *Nursery World* magazine there was an advertisement for Chilprufe underwear (little kids sporting in their long woollen combinations): young readers were invited to colour it in and try to win a prize. She leaned over my shoulder to show me how to do it, and *coloured it all in*. It was sent in, and I won the prize. But it wasn't *winning*. And a third, worse, thing: the girls at school were pointing at me and laughing – 'You've got rouge on!'. I denied it furiously, crying. But I remembered later that after brushing my hair she'd been rubbing something into my cheeks, in front of a mirror that I couldn't see.

I know these things should be no more than a joke. What a critical child, what sharp eyes! But it was important and terrible. Truth was either truth or nothing. These were falsities, encroachments, obliterations.

A mixed-up childhood then, which I finally envisage with two deep crevasses in it. One was the seriously mad nanny that my mother admitted had taken over during an absence: I have no memory of this at all, but my brother remembers screaming until rescued by Lily, our head parlourmaid.

And the other crevasse? I only heard about it many years later. 'You used to run away', my father mentioned gruffly. 'And no one could persuade you to come home except me.' *Run away*? No memory of it at all? Why? Where? And he was perfectly *compos mentis*. No, I didn't ask about it. One never did.

(iii)

One of the places where my parents often went for holidays was Blickling in Norfolk, home of Lord Lothian. He had been General Secretary to the Rhodes Trust since before our installation in Rhodes House, a leading figure in administering the legacy. As anyone will know who has visited Blickling in the many years since it was taken over by the National Trust, it is a magnificent Tudor building with deer park, manicured gardens, and – in my day, at any rate – a ghost in a sealed tower. Lothian (my parents always called him this rather than his given name of Philip) was, I understand, from one of those great old English Catholic families – though he had, oddly, switched over to Christian Science as an adult. He is someone I truly remember with affection. Rhodes Trust people – Lord This and Sir That – were part of the scenery, but he was different. Possibly he even saved my life. Going through my father's papers recently, I found a letter from Lothian to my mother written at a time when I was very ill. It is dated August 1935. 'I have never talked to you about Christian Science', he wrote to her, 'because long experience has shown me that pressing religious opinions does more harm than good':

> But it is so clear to those who understand it that fear is the root of nearly all illness and conflict... I hope that this last operation may mean localization of the poison and may free the rest of her system.

THE LONG VACATION

The strongest influence is the mother's. If you can keep from being afraid, still more if you can see that Rosemary lives in God – Eternal Life – not the poor little body we look at but the spirit of which the least we can see in her is the faint outline, you will do more for her life and recovery than even the doctors can do. I am doing what I can for you both.

God bless you all.

Some months later, I wrote to ask him to my eighth birthday party. He replied with sweet courtesy that he would have loved to come, but had some much more boring matters to see to.

So I did recover. By luck, or by doctoring, or by prayer?

While I was in hospital, I would look down over Marylebone and see, far below, tiny people walking the pavements, crossing roads, putting up umbrellas; there was a whole other world out there, I grasped, going on just as if nothing had happened, as if all ordinary life hadn't ceased. Strange! And outside were the plane trees, leaning in the wind with their little globes twirling, which for years meant London and illness to me.

A fine production of *Macbeth* that I saw recently found a way, for audiences who no longer believe in witches, of putting back the horror into the play. The curtain went up on a hospital recovery room, dimly lit, with silent witch-nurses manipulating motionless patients. A patient who tried to sit up was held down. And I remembered trying, in such a place, to pull the oxygen mask off my face and always having it pushed back by someone unseen.

THE LONG VACATION

Or I was on a trolley, going down in a lift – I asked the nurse where we were going 'To the ante-room,' she said. She stood at the head of the trolley, and I leaned my head against her breast. It was so soft, so warm, starchy and crackly too. When, later, I was with my mother visiting some child in hospital, I looked down at her, quite small and pale, in the bed and thought, 'I know where you are, you're in that Other Place,' and turned my head away.

The tickling of threads, pulled deliciously slowly from the edge of the bandage round my head.

They asked me what I would like to eat and I said, 'Pineapple.' They brought a big, prickly thing that was a disappointment. Of course, I'd meant ordinary pineapple, from a tin.

After I came out of hospital my mother and I had a strange convalescent stay at Blickling: the servants were on holiday, a fierce wind howled round the Tudor chimneys, and I nearly cut my thumb off trying to open up a banana. I have the scar still. On oak-panelled walls ancestral portraits looked hostile; it was splendidly eerie. Some time later I was allowed to stay when there was a party of grown-up guests. In spite of my – in some ways – privileged way of life, this is the only time I ever glimpsed the real aristocratic country house life of the 1930s. Breakfast I particularly remember. It was on a long side table with starched linen tablecloths: under one highly polished silver dome would be devilled kidneys, under another scrambled eggs and bacon, and kippers, perhaps, under another. Somewhere, flunkies lurked.

Lothian went to the States in 1939 as British Ambassador. While he was there he got some kind of serious illness and, as a Christian Scientist, I suppose didn't see a doctor. He died in 1940 at the age of 52. From what I've read, he was not the weak appeaser of Nazism that has been suggested – but that's quite another story. When he died I was also across the Atlantic, as a war evacuee in Canada. I hardly grasped the death. Everything at the time seemed to have died or collapsed or be too far away.

Meanwhile, back in 1936, I was eight years old. Some people, I suppose, were unaware that another world war was looming; many, including my parents, were very well aware. Even I knew that something was up. We had a German governess at the time – rather a nice one, compared to her predecessor. '*Wasch die Hände*' before meals, she taught us, and '*kämm die Haar*'. Who was this bad Hitler person they talked about, I asked Brigitte on one of our interminable health-giving walks through the university parks. 'Oh, he's not so bad at all', she said. 'He's done wonders for us in dealing with the Jews'. I wasn't a stupid child. I took note.

And the Rhodes machine, in these pre-war times? The legacy of the South African Hitler who said, 'I prefer land to niggers' as he grabbed another slice of prime territory? As early 1910 E. M. Forster had written in *Howard's End* that 'the imperialist is not what he thinks or seems. He is a destroyer... Though his ambitions may be fulfilled, the Earth that he inherits will be grey'. Yet my impression is that in the 1930s there was something left of the imperial dream; though much updated and sanitized. It was not that we were lectured at home or school on the glory of empire. There was still, I think, an Empire Day, but I never remember it being celebrated. (In Caribbean schools, I discovered later when working in Dominica, it went on being taught for years.) A lot of the world map was pink, of course – but that was just natural, as speaking English was natural.

The Rhodes Trust, at any rate, was apparently flourishing, but evolving.[5] The original South African cabal had now died off, though a lingering wish to swamp the pesky Dutch with fine British stock remained. The shipping out of cargoes of British ladies, presumably marriageable and certainly white, was even supported by various organisations. (I wonder what happened to these ladies?) Schools – white and anglophone – were supported. In Oxford, the university was at times uneasy about the imperialist Trojan horse in their midst. Some parts of the empire were sending in sensible chaps on their scholarships, some apparently not. Jamaica was tricky, so was Bermuda; Malta was granted scholarships, so that it would not be tempted into un-British ways. India was under consideration but posed problems.

The German scholarships that Rhodes had so oddly set up after his chat with the Kaiser were again to be discontinued. But from the period between the wars, when they were in operation, it was a German Scholar – the

---

[5] I am indebted here to *The History of the Rhodes Trust*, edited by Anthony Kenny, a former Warden of Rhodes House. It is amazing, some seventy years later, to trace out these threads about which I knew so little.

brave and tragic Adam von Trott[6] – who took part in the failed assassination plot against Hitler. He was hanged for this in 1944. During my gap year, as it would now be called, I met his widow in Caux above Montreux in Switzerland. Here she had found a haven in the headquarters of the Oxford Group, otherwise known as 'Moral Rearmament', a cultish Christian movement set up by Frank Buchman. It had a reputation for eccentric public confessions – perhaps a forerunner of encounter groups? – but seemed disappointingly normal. I managed to find out very little from her about her husband, alas, but she seemed well cared for. Being an aristocrat and of course an 'Aryan', he had had no difficulty in leaving Germany to take up his scholarship, as Jewish students did.

Did I, as a child, know anything of all this? Not in the slightest. Rhodes stuff was all just parental stuff to be ignored or rebelled against. Later in my teens, if there were Rhodes Scholars about the house, I disdained them as hulking South African athletes – being myself, of course, more in the Sartre and Kafka line at that time. Rhodes had been very keen on promoting manly sporting chaps; I've discovered with pleasure that the reason my father, before he ever came to England, failed to gain a Rhodes Scholarship himself was that, though he scored 18 out of 20 for intellect and the same for character, he only achieved 2 out of 20 for sport. Well done! – an excellent sense of proportion. And to think that he had, in Australia, had his nose broken by a cricket ball, giving him a rather distinguished hauteur.

---

[6] G. MacDonogh: *A Good German.* Letters page, New York Review of Books, 444. 5 (1997)

THE LONG VACATION

I feel sorry now that neither in childhood, nor later on, did I make much attempt to know about the institution that provided our bread and butter and extremely stately home – and my riding lessons and ballet lessons and fencing lessons. And roller skates and visits to the pantomime and Red Indian costume and a churchgoing straw hat trimmed with buttercups. Nor, later, did I go out of my way to congratulate my father on his knighthood, or read anything of a non-legal kind that he wrote. These are the regrets of old age. Only now, rescuing his dusty papers from the cellar, am I properly looking through a schoolboy poem , 'Job'; two jokey novels in the style of the 1920s; two plays that were never staged.

* * * *

Meanwhile, Oxford High School dragged on and war, half-realised even by a child, grew nearer.

The head of the leading clique was a girl called Ursula, and she didn't like me; this was very horrible. Then the lovely Burn twins, Joey and Molly, arrived and became my best friends. Their gym knickers were *extremely* neat, and they could do wonderful handstands. So my school memories are more of popularity fluctuations than of charismatic teachers and intellectual enlightenment. The twins come into my dreams sometimes, standing in the distance. I'm told they have Alzheimer's now.

Hockey was horrible, certainly. But there was riding in the New Forest (anxiety kicking in again – jodhpurs too baggy), climbing a certain copper beech in the Parks that is *still there*, shopping from the ice-white dairy lined with tiles of milkmaids (now a Peruvian boutique). And adoring Leslie Howard.

It was real, this adoration – I am not being coy and indulgent – I loved the look and sound of the man, and still do. The vulnerability of the steep brow and sensuality of sleepy eyelids... The voice. As an evacuee I took with me a picture of him torn out of the cook's magazine, and was stunned by his death in a plane crash. Of course I saw him in *The Scarlet Pimpernel*; one of my favourite books ('They seek him here, / They seek him there, / Those Frenchies seek him everywhere'). I have seen him in love with Ingrid Bergman, seen his cigarette smoke drifting out into the darkness as he whispered 'I shall be back.' And sometimes he *is* back, when they show the old films – and I feel just the same.[7]

That pre-war winter was a cold, cold one. The meadow flanking the Cherwell by the Japanese bridge was flooded by a foot or two and froze. People clumped through the ice but I, brilliantly, walked on it and was admired. I was very light. War stalked nearer. Years later, Leslie Howard's death was to be explained: the Germans had believed that Churchill was the celebrity passenger on the plane they shot down.

It must have been that spring that there was the last Rhodes House fancy dress ball in the Milner Hall, and I was allowed to come down for a while. Some kindly gentleman walked me solemnly round the floor. We

---

[7] I know: he was rubbish in *Gone with the Wind*. But the part required it.

schoolgirls were beginning to think about dancing: the 'Lambeth Walk'; the 'Hokey-Cokey', the beginnings of ballroom (girls in pairs) to the sound of 'The Sweetest Song in the World' (we had a very rude version of this), a class on the waltz and the polka. And ballet, of course, which I can still feel in my spine and my fingertips.

I was making up my first dress, in blue-flowered cotton, Oxford High's summer uniform. My brother and I were now allowed to eat downstairs with the grown-ups, and a sweet Swiss girl replaced the dragon governess. When my parents made the odd decision to take us, on the brink of war, to our first holiday abroad – beside one of the Normandy beaches that would be devastated five years later – Jacqueline came with us, and there was a moment of sadness when she left for the safety of Switzerland. This rather dangerous holiday should be interesting to record – but do I remember any more of it? No. Only the excruciation of asking for an ice cream in French: embarrassment always the one unforgettable emotion. I'm told that we returned on one of the last available Channel boats – but is this a family myth?

At home we children still had to drink tepid Ovaltine and go early to bed, where I lay awake worrying. Could I have caught infantile paralysis? (This was the name then for polio.) Could I breathe, really breathe, or was there a sort of catch, a weight, something odd about my thudding heart? I knew that schools and swimming-pools had been closed down, that children with the illness were shut up inside an 'iron lung'. For ever. And even if I did survive, how would I ever manage to be grown-up? It looked so difficult; who would show me how? What job would I be able to do? Surely not a teacher, or a nurse. Perhaps a vet? A bookseller? Could I be lucky enough to get someone to marry me, and avoid the whole job problem? I already deeply but doubtingly hoped for this. I wore a ring from a Christmas cracker on my left hand: I was 'engaged'. But who to? In a Cathedral garden a kindly clergyman asked me about the ring, but I ran away and wouldn't answer. It was a secret, so secret that even I didn't know the answer. From another cracker I got a little card that you had to rub with a wet finger to see the face of your future husband. I licked and rubbed, and a face dimly, excitingly appeared. I sent off for a free sample tin of Noxema face cream: it was pink, and smelt like toffee.

I was eleven. So round about now, war with Germany was finally declared.

I have no memory of... but wait. Wasn't I in the garden, on the lawn, and they came out from listening to the radio – no, the *wireless* – and told me?

My brother and I were immediately sent off to a kind of temporary evacuation at a friend's farm. Was instant bombardment expected, sudden invasion? At the farm there were hay barns to hide in and a raft to launch on the duck pond. But almost at once I was struck by an agonising homesickness for Oxford, a pain that made me gasp. Why wasn't I wise enough, a year later when the question of real evacuation came up, to realise how much worse this would be if the Atlantic separated me from home for years? When the day soon came for us to be fetched back from the farm, nothing warlike having yet happened, I walked miles along the road to meet the family car. The wait for it was like, some twenty years later, when I was an analysand, the space between the street corner and the doorbell beside the analyst's door. I ran then, I leaped up the front steps. But before my hand reached the bell, the gap was fathoms deep.

* * * *

Pam, Barbara, Vivienne and Joan: the London evacuees arrived! The government had prepared plans for instant evacuation of schoolchildren from vulnerable areas. Oxford was safer than London, though Canada came to be safer still. Everyone knows the photographs: small bewildered children lined up at railway stations, each child with boxed gas mask over shoulder. 'Got your gas mask?' was the slogan put about, like 'Is your journey really necessary?' at stations, and 'Walls have ears' (disguised Nazis perhaps listening to our chat). Why in fact was there no poison gas attack? My father, in his war, went through that very unpleasant one. A mist blew over the field that withered the grass and turned his buttons and his silver cigarette case green.

The girls from Kensington High School who came to live with us were not small children, but around or above my own age. For me, it was all fun and excitement. They called me Fuzzy (the hair!) and marvelled that water came out of our taps hot enough to fill hot water bottles. How else could you fill them?, I asked. 'Boil a kettle', they chorused, I gasped: all the way down to the scullery, braving cook and kitchenmaids, to carry up water? It was not long since

I had assumed that hot water came out of taps just as the cold did, from some central source.

But they were sophisticated, the Kensington girls. None of them tied their hair back with a scrap of elastic, or wore their brothers' outsize socks slipping around their ankles. One of them put *curl papers* in her hair at night. One had lived in London in a *maisonette!* – something I'd never heard of, though my French was good. Some stayed on with us, one disappeared home quickly, one became a friend for life. One buttered my mother up and became a favourite, another had a mind of her own and earned disfavour.

This was the time of the 'phoney war' for us. Oxford had few air raids: only twice before I went away did we go down to the cellar at the sound of that hateful *whoo-whoo*. Once it must have been a practice run to see that we knew what to do; once, a stray German plane returning from a more important target jettisoning bombs in a field. Nothing to cause fright. And yet I do find the sound of a whole mass of planes droning overhead very unpleasant.

Sirens. Gas masks. Ration cards. Vera Lynn. Food queues. Who hasn't heard it all? My granddaughter has even learned it at school. 'We've done World War Two', she says. And she's only seven.

Meanwhile of course the university and the Rhodes Trust were going through upheavals like everything else. Some Scholars got home, some chose to stay in England: Americans, this early in the war, were free. English boys were being called up into the Forces; some of them, medical students in particular, could continue their courses. Some women were joining the Forces, others were directed into war work in factories or on farms. A smart housemaid left, and one of the kitchenmaids. It was all in a piecemeal way, grasped by me, as was the advance of German armies across Europe. Yet I think – but am not sure – that I didn't truly grasp that these armies could arrive in Dover or Southend and advance by tank and plane and bomb towards London. And then Oxford.

So I believe it was indeed unexpected, that question at lunchtime one Sunday in 1940. My father was cutting slices of greyish wartime bread. He had just cut a piece and was dividing it in quarters, one for each of us. Holding the breadknife in hand, he asked me if I would like to go to the United States.

An invitation from Yale University, he said. A group to be got together of university children from Oxford. Parents meetings being organized at Rhodes House to make arrangements.

The twins were going. I said 'yes'.

2. Leaving home

> The child in a foster-home (or institution) is living in two worlds, the foster-home (or institution) and his own home... However good the foster-mother or house-mother, the child will regard her as a more or less poor makeshift for his own mother, to be left as soon as possible.
>
> John Bowlby, *Child Care and the Growth of Love*

THE LONG VACATION

I didn't realise then how many ex-Rhodes Scholars were involved in the offer to take us Oxford children: Professor Fulton of Yale, Professor Cairns in Oxford, Howard Florey, of penicillin fame, Dean Lowe of Christ Church; he whose sermons my mother always managed to evade. My father was contacted and took on the leadership of the committee. Of this organising I know nothing. It was just wartime; the Germans were evil; there was danger, for city children had already been sent to the countryside.

A contemporary of mine was more realistic: he tells me he bought a German dictionary and buried his Boy Scout uniform under a hedge.

A government scheme for overseas evacuation was temporarily set up, until the sinking of the *City of Benares*. The increasing number of German submarines seems scarcely to have been realised.[8]

It was many years later that my father said casually: 'We didn't know whether we should send you to Canada. But you were a very difficult girl.' I've been pondering the implications ever since.

It was July when our ship sailed out of Liverpool. As I remember it, it was nevertheless a cold day, damp and blowy up on deck. The *Antonia* was set for Canada, across who knows how many miles of shifting icy water, with a good many enemy submarines in it. I have no picture of watching the English shore fade out of sight. Something, as usual, has blotted that out.

---

[8] Micheal Fethney: *The Absurd and the Brave*

But I do remember the time between the decision and that departure day. It was so short: just a matter of days spent in hurried preparations. Nobody was cross with me, even when I came down at night asking for an apple because I couldn't sleep.

My brother was not to go, because he was three years younger. People – Miss Fathers and others – were pushed towards sewing machines to run up clothes that would be suitable for cold and hot un-English climates. A blue 'sun suit' with white spots (it soon grew embarrassingly tight). A green wool dress with blanket-stitch embroidery. A skimpy navy skirt and jacket. (Strange that when I forget all else, I can always remember clothes.) I was taken up to London to Lillywhites on Regent Street to buy a checked anorak and baggy snow-proof trousers. There must have been a family round-up of clothes coupons: rationing was surely in force by then. These new clothes, though, proved to be somehow eccentrically wrong when I reached the other side of the Atlantic.

To give the parents a farewell present, I asked if I could have £5 from my moneybox. From Blackwell's I got a rather lovely book about Oxford: I have it still myself, among the other 3,000 or so of my books. 'To Mummy and Daddy, with love from Rosemary'. When I was back home, some years later, my father said, 'We felt so guilty when we found you'd bought that book for us.' (Why?)

Actually it's a book I should have given to myself, for remembrance's sake; over the years away in Canada, unwillingly, I began to lose grasp of Oxford, though nothing firmly took its place. I tried reading books about the history of it, and looking at illustrations, but nothing quite worked. For an essay competition at the new school, later on, I wrote a description of Oxford: it didn't win. Quite right. I had lost the connection.

Anyway, new clothes packed, leaving my mother embarrassingly crying on Oxford station, I went with our group on the Liverpool train. It was a long slow journey; wartime trains weren't to be relied on. Adults who were with us complained of feeling dirty, as smuts from the steam engine blew in. I said proudly, 'I love being dirty!'. It was all going to be exciting, all an adventure.

The only craft I had been on up to then was a punt on the Cherwell – and the little Channel ferry after our French holiday, of course. The *Antonia* was no punt. It seemed enormous – deck on deck, ladder on ladder, corridor on corridor. It was certainly overcrowded, with adults as well as child refugees and mothers with babies. I was in a cabin with my three schoolfriends: to say that *that* was overcrowded would be an understatement – it was pure Marx Brothers. (That hilarious scene where person after person crowds into a ship's cabin while the steward doggedly makes up the bunks). Our stewards were very nice to us girls, and my friend Joey delighted in sitting up for them in her top bunk, half dressed and with her (so far) totally flat chest on view.

Outside the cabins there was running, banging, shouting, squealing of babies. And of course the throb, on and on, of the engines. We were far down in the ship.

There was an area, not quite a dining-room, where tables were set up for us to eat in shifts. The first meal must have been breakfast, for I clearly remember that we were served buckwheat pancakes. Delicious! A novel food already:

must remember buckwheat, I thought – take it on board, as it were. (Ha!) But soon eating stopped.

Seasickness, almost unrelenting for much of the ten days, the only relief sips of water and bits of dry biscuit. Can I describe it? Can anyone? You either know it or you don't. Just writing down the 's' word makes me feel queasy. Like childbirth without the splendid finale, it is an enormity. Nowadays there are very good pills to be taken; then there was only a remedy called 'Mothersills', which sounded cosy but was totally ineffectual. During our passage, I believe there was some particularly massive storm. I must have dragged myself up on deck once at least, because I remember looking at a wall of water approaching and thinking, 'But that's impossible. That's as big as a two-storey house. Not possible'. It was possible.

Being on deck was in any case dangerous without being attached to a line. Mostly the days were spent in our airless, vibrating cabin. I think I was the sickest of us four – but maybe I was just oblivious of what was happening to anybody else. Not knowing or caring. Ideas about adventure, travel, excitement vanished now and didn't come back.

There was a rumour one day that a depth charge had just missed us by inches. I wonder if it was true? If it had been, and the torpedo had hit us, I would probably not be here to write. The armed escort had left us some 800 miles out. What happened to the children on the *City of Benares* would have happened to us. I want to put their story down here.

The *Benares* left Britain for Canada on September 13th 1940, some six weeks after the *Antonia*. There had already been U-boat attacks and partial sinkings, but a government-sponsored evacuation scheme, controversially, was still sending batches of children out. Some six hundred miles out into the Atlantic without Royal Navy protection, the *Benares* was struck by a 500lb torpedo. Some of those aboard, including thirty children, were killed at once by the force of the explosion. They were the luckier ones.

Many more children died during a confused attempt to launch lifeboats. Some were tipped out of the tilted boats into the sea where they died quickly in the icy water; some fell from ropes in trying to reach the boats. The lifeboats that did float were still half full of water, and in these, the smallest first, most children died of exposure and shock, slipping over the side into the water. It was some twenty hours before any rescue approached those still surviving; one boat that held survivors was at sea for eight days before rescue. As well as floating bodies, rescuers found lifeboats that were afloat but with no passengers left alive in them. Of the remaining children that were saved, three never recovered and were 'buried' at sea.

* * * *

That is what didn't happen to us.

We had been nearly two weeks at sea when we first sighted land. Wonderful moment: we approached and sailed up the St Lawrence river, where we could see real trees, real houses, even real people. We docked at

Montreal, where we were shepherded into a large empty hall and spent the night on straw palliasses on the floor.

The next morning I was called into an office, where a man sat at a desk with lists of names. 'There's a bit of a problem here', he said. 'Your arrival seems to be expected by two different families. You could go down to the States with the others, or you could go to the Micheners in Toronto. It's up to you, really.'

It must have been a warm day: what I remember is the damp patches under the arms of my cotton frock. The Micheners: I knew about them – they were friends of my parents, some kind of Rhodes Trust people, who had visited England. They lived on a hill, I had once been told, and had three daughters. In my mind I saw a bright snowy hill for sliding down. And sisters. That they knew my parents seemed to bring me closer to home, for which I was already feeling the dull pervading longing that I knew was going to get worse. I made a wrong decision.

'I'm not coming with you. I'm going to Toronto', I said to the twins.

That I made a wrong decision shouldn't cast any slur on the Micheners. But if I had gone with the schoolmates I think I would have fared better, suffered less shock and loneliness.

When I reached Toronto I found that they were on holiday. I was taken to some friends of theirs who kindly put me into their guest room. I lay in bed while the room heaved up and down around me. I was sick, I think. I was still at sea.

THE LONG VACATION

How long was I there? Perhaps only a week or two. When I was leaving, my hosts said it had been lovely to have me, and we would keep in touch. I never saw them again, nor even know their name now.

* * * *

The first arrival at the Micheners' house I don't remember. Toronto was hot, I know, and smelled to me of petrol – perhaps because, due to petrol rationing, Oxford hadn't. The house I came to know so well was indeed on a hill – not a glowing mountain as I had visualized it, but on a leafy, suburban sloping road. A fine north American detached house with a front porch, a garden, and a good many bedrooms. A brick path and steep steps led down to the sidewalk (no, not *pavement*) that in winter had to be shovelled clear of many inches of snow.

My three 'foster' sisters were five, eight and around my own age –this one was my almost-sister Joan, who was the best thing about my stay. Joan and I were to share a bedroom. Its pinkish wallpaper with tiny silver stars amazed me after the solid but pale furnishings at home. And the closets (again, not wardrobes) were miniature rooms, which one could step into and close the door. There was one in the guest room that I went into to cry; no one must see me cry. The pain of homesickness didn't stop.

'This is my little English war guest', my foster mother would say, bringing me down into the drawing-room to stand in front of her guests. 'When she arrived she was only 90 pounds and now she's 120!'

How to describe the newness, the strangeness, the refugee-ness that I rapidly acquired? Wrong clothes, strange stuffy accent – the sisters laughed at me, but not too unkindly. In my later wanderings among psychoanalysts I often found myself saying, 'I don't know where I am or who I am'. None of them ever asked me what I meant.

I was desperately anxious to conform. I learned things quickly: not just 'sidewalk' and 'closet' but sneakers, panties, candy, garbage can, bobby-pins and lots more – painfully unlearned three years later in the face of English derision. I still have trouble with the English 'dustbin', though. What dust? What are you supposed to call garbage?

I learned in frosty Canada not to open windows (double ones) in winter, nor mosquito screens in summer. I learned to hang up my pyjamas on a peg rather than fold them under the pillow ('We don't do that in Canada: it's unhealthy'). I learned to wear fur-edged snow boots, ear muffs, an interlined coat, to use Kleenex tissues rather than embroidered handkerchiefs. I learned 'She'll be Comin' Round the Mountain' instead of 'The Lambeth Walk' and 'Run, Adolph, Run'; 'The Old Grey Mare, She Ain't What She Used to Be' rather than 'Hitler Has Only Got One Ball...

And Goebbels
Has no balls
AT ALL.

THE LONG VACATION

(As a matter of fact, I think I only knew that one later.) I learned that poison ivy stings and that there is an illness called hives. I learned foods: maple sugar (heavenly), peanut butter, angel food cake, peaches as a familiar dessert rather than a rare hothouse fruit. I learned to skate, to pick up dimes from the bottom of a swimming pool. Once we went out in the car with our clumping wooden skis (wearing the mittens from Lillywhites) and were pulled along by the car holding on to ropes – an exciting preparation for skiing later in Switzerland and Austria.

I learned 'The Maple Leaf for Ever' and, later, 'The Star-Spangled Banner'. I learned that fridge doors must be kept shut – I had never seen the actual inside of a fridge before. I learned, to my embarrassment, that grown-up people could go around naked in the bathroom; and, even more shocking, was made by my sisters to go shoplifting for candy.

I learned cinema! Almost as soon as I arrived at my new home I was sent off with Joan to see a film called *All This and Heaven Too*. With Bette Davis. Amazing.

* * * *

Here I have to cover a period of three years, of which I have less memory than any other period of my life. My memory went peculiar then, went crooked.

I didn't, I think, know *what* I knew, what remembered, what I hoped for. I don't know whether I was aware of much about the war, knew that the Blitz on London had started; whether we listened to war news on the radio, or read any of it in the Toronto *Globe and Mail*; whether I speculated much about when I would be home again, or what would happen if the Axis won the war and occupied Britain. I had a locket with a tiny photo of my parents in it, but I don't think I wore it.

About a year after arriving, I was sent down on a holiday to the States, where I could meet up with my dear twin friends. This was lovely, and I have cheerful photos of it. On the train back north, a kind lady accompanying me said, 'You seem to have lost your pep, Rosemary'. I was aware that I was putting on a 'lost-my-pep' face, that I wanted it noticed. But something truly was lost, some thread of connection broken at about this time, and left to be washed over by a dead ocean.

Don't think I forget that, not long before, London children aged anything from three or four had been packed into trains with their gas masks and just a name label, to arrive at villages and be picked at random by doubtful hosts. And before that, children from Europe put onto grimmer trains destined for England, leaving behind families they would never see again.

* * * *

There were things so *missing* in this other home, as well as family. Not just the bells every quarter-hour, or Christ Church quad on a sunny Sunday morning, or the copper beech tree, or roller skates or Clark's sandals or Webbers' school uniform department, but books. My new home was a well-to-do one and I'm sure there were books, but I don't remember that I read anything during those years. In particular, poetry wasn't there. Perhaps that's why the poems I was thinking about before I left, are still sharp to me:

> When we were all asleep the snow came falling.
> In large white flakes upon the city brown –

There was an icy winter the year before I left Oxford and in my inner sight I saw these flakes falling in St Giles, in the dark, somewhere near the Judge's Lodgings. Snow there certainly was in Canada, whole feet of it, but not this mysterious descent. (It is by Robert Bridges and called 'London Snow'.)

I had been chanting to myself, too: 'Sabrina fair, listen where thou art sitting / Under the glassy cool translucent wave...'. This had something to do with the turquoise seas and skies on the postcards my parents sent home from the French Riviera. Another line was 'Magic casements, opening on the foam of faery lands forlorn...'. The book had a black woodcut illustrating this, always a scary thing. I think that image goes back to when I still half-believed in fairy stuff, and felt I could look right through the dark casement towards it.

Pictures, too: I had had a book in my Oxford bookcase called *The World's Hundred Best Paintings*. It doesn't sound very sophisticated, and reproductions then were poor, but whoever gave it to me made an inspired choice. I pored

THE LONG VACATION

long over the plates, and I think the book foreshadowed my collecting paintings in later life. There was a Michelangelo *tondo*, wasn't there? And van Eyck's dear Arnolfini couple: why was his hat so big? And her belly so round? What breed was the little dog with the human face?

But there is a special chink of light, of poetry, that dates from the Toronto time. At school we were divided into competitive groups, and tried to win points for our own. Learning things by heart gained points, and as I had no truck with hockey sticks and such, my contribution was to learn the whole of Keats' *Ode to a Nightingale*. I loved its opening sense of a damp, half-moonlit English orchard. Some fifty years later, in Hammersmith's beautiful Victorian public library, a very old black man was for some reason quoting from the *Ode*. I joined in! – and, triumphantly, we repeated the whole poem in unison. Perfect.

It is easier – I don't know why – to evoke the bad times than such very special good ones. Words are so hard to find for the good ones; and exposing them on a page seems to send them out, vulnerable, into danger.

* * * *

At some point during the Canada years there was a transatlantic phone call to my parents laid on for me. I had been told that there was a cable running *under the ocean*, connecting Canada and England. This still seems to me

81

extraordinary, more so than lines bounced off satellites somewhere in outer space. That cable! A thick whitish-grey snake, I thought. Did it lie on the sea bed, on sand, with actual miles of empty water above it? Who dropped it down there, and how? Were there fishes (we did once, on the *Antonia*, see a whale spouting on the horizon). I felt that my squeaky and faltering words, my Canadian accent, hardly managed to run right along that great snaky cable to a far-distant home. I don't know what we said. Or tried to say.

'If you come home with a Canadian accent, we'll send you right back again!', had been said with blustery laughter before I left.

That was the English snobbery I've mentioned earlier. It didn't just extend to the comical under-classes whose vowels weren't quite right, but – in spite of the great Rhodes togetherness dream – to 'colonials' and their funny ways. My father must himself have started out with the Australian twang and hastened to lose it (thought, oddly, the only time I noticed it was groping through the blackout at Victoria station on my return). My Canadian 'mother', an elegant and accomplished woman, had been to Britain more than once on Rhodes visits. They had stayed at Blickling, I know, among the toffs, and there she must have been haughtily condescended to. She was the last person to take kindly to this: Canadians, at that time, felt condescended to by both the English and the Americans. I think I was half aware of this even at the time. There was much about 'We don't do that in Canada' (put our knickers in the top drawer rather than the bottom one, things of that sort.) Between her and my mother, a prickly woman herself, a sense of rivalry developed. It may have started with that oft-repeated mantra, 'She was only 92 pounds when I got her, and now she's 110!'. My main value to my mother (as I felt in my bad moments) was as demonstration of her excellent care; but what she had sent across the Atlantic was not just a lazy, sulky teenager, but one who had been diagnosed on arrival as 'suffering from malnutrition'. Malnutrition! Who wouldn't be skinny and weak after two weeks of vomiting? Photographs show that I was always a pretty normal shape, even a nice one.

So long ago, all this, and yet so present. Slicing up mushrooms last night, I remembered my Canadian father taking us all out into frosty northern woods to pick them; we came back with a big puffball, and deliciously sliced and fried it. The skating lessons, the orthodontic bills. A special trip to Niagara Falls. There were clothes for me from refugee parcels, smelling of sweat – but then the surprise of a brand-new red handbag with a matching 'beanie' (little round cap). Red velvet, with a feather.

The psychologist John Bowlby, quoted in my epigraph, says that the child in substitute care is living in two worlds, 'the foster-home and his own home'. That this went on being true of me, an oddity from my own memory shows. During some argument with my sorely tried foster-family, they had asked, 'How did you know it was four o'clock?' – or six or eight, whatever it was. 'By the bells, of course', I said. Bells? In Toronto? Or the bells of Tom Tower, Merton, Keble, St Mary the Virgin?

I did in the end, live in only the one, the current new world that surrounded me. But by then something essential was lost.

THE LONG VACATION

* * *

For two of the Toronto summers I was sent up north to a girls' summer camp by the lakes: I had been taken to thank some benefactor who was paying for this. The lakes of Ontario are not anything like our own gentle Wordsworthian ones. They are vast and aloof, bleak sometimes and dense with pine forest, stretching off into a misty distance where perhaps a portage[9] will connect with another string of lakes, and then another. Human settlements in these great spaces are humble and few and, further north, may be reachable only by air. Our settlement of wooden cabins, dining hall and workshops was built along the side of one of these lakes, and a camp for boys (in which, as yet, I had no interest) was further off on the other side.

I loved all this. It was everything I had wanted Canada to be: wildness, remoteness, a hint of a redskin past, a danger that moose or beaver or bear might be in the forest, strange evening bird cries from the loon and the whipoorwill. It made up for not being allowed to join a Girl Guide group in the city: this wilderness was the real thing. My reading of John Buchan fed into it, and the popular talks of pigtailed Archie, alias Grey Owl, and even the South African *veld* yarns in my uncles' books at Park Town. Here it really mattered that you swim well, have a

---

[9] A portage is where the canoe is lifted and carried overland to the next launching place.

sharp knife, and know now to make up a camp fire. Baden-Powell himself would have been proud of me! Round these fires we had camp songs to sing:

> Anyone can see
> What's troubling me –
> I'm longing for the northern Pines,

I would hum nostalgically, back in the city.

Here for the first time since I came to Canada, I had friends. There were six of us in my cabin and, as girls do, we chattered on until late at night. Perhaps I did belong to the human race after all, was my feeling. I wasn't invisible! In the city once, stepping onto a streetcar, I heard someone across the road cheerfully shouting my name. Impossible: who would do that? It was a girl from camp, on a visit to Toronto: someone from that other world.

If only my letters home hadn't been thrown away... Not that I want material to write about, but just to know better what was going on for me then – *where* I was and *who* I was.

There was a certain a certain settling-down, there were letters from home eagerly, eagerly waited for. Big chunks (of what?) had usually been cut out by the censors. And next, of course, there was school.

I was sent to a private day school for girls with Joan, though I think I wouldn't have minded an ordinary Canadian school. Because of Oxford High School's standards, I was soon put into a higher class than Joan's. She didn't complain. I knew that this must be an expensive place, with its big grounds and sports field, unlike cramped little Oxford High. I was always half-aware that I *cost money*. For dentistry as well as school fees: the Canadian dentist, had looked appalled at my English teeth and fixed braces on them. Mr Pegler of Oxford, with his Gilbert-and-Sullivan hums and the clanking great drill and laughing-gas that kept me sleepless in fear beforehand, hadn't got it right.

School wasn't happy. Being a couple of years younger than the girls in my class, I was – not bullied at all – just ignored. In any class of girls there is a pecking order. At the top of the order in my class were girls who wore Air Force pins from boyfriends, hummed the tunes of Harry James's glorious trumpet ('You made me love you, I didn't wanna do it'), and stood in front of mirrors saying mysterious things to each other like 'D'you really think he...?' and 'Oh boy, last night...'. At the bottom of our pecking order there were three of us: myself, damningly known to be 'brainy'; Jane, bright but a dwarf, about four and a half feet high; and Barbara, who had a tragic rash of pimples or warts over her face. Because there were three of us, I could sometimes find a companion to eat my packed lunch with. But not always.

I didn't in any case have school friends to bring home, because on Saturdays I did the family's ironing. This seems fair enough, but I thought it very Cinderella, and mooched about the house crooning, in gospel fashion, 'Sometimes I feel like a motherless child, oh yes Lord.' There was a room for ironing, and down below in the substantial cellar that Canadian houses had for the furnace heating the building, were deep sinks and scrubbing-boards for the washing.

The teaching at school must have been good: before I left for home in 1943 I passed some Canadian examination that exonerated me from taking Higher Certificate in England. Maths, as usual, nearly betrayed me: I seem to remember that a basic pass was 50% but I scrambled through with 49%. History was Canadian history – rather scanty and dull, mostly fur trappers and snowy wastes – so I have never had a grasp of English history, beyond colouring in gentlemen in doublets and hose.

Teachers there are more memorable to me now than my schoolmates in their green tunics, bunched at the waist St-Trinian's-fashion to show black-stockinged thighs. There was a Latin teacher, Eton-cropped, steel-haired and steel-nerved, who should have been preserved on film as a teaching aid. A class would fall silent at the sound of Miss Ellis's approaching footsteps; before she had reached the door we would be standing motionless by our desks. Her entrance was slow and hieratic, her glance took in every face, and by the time she pronounced, 'You may sit down', the class was weak with terror. Latin remained unlearnable, though.

It was a joy to me that I could go on with ballet lessons, in a class directed by Boris Volkov of the Canadian Ballet (yes, there was one). With joy came worry – always the strongest memory – that when I stretched backwards from the barre I would pop right out of the top of my tutu. Nevertheless, I think of ballet discipline as just about the most worthwhile part of my education after reading and writing. The sensation of bourrée-ing on points across a polished floor is what life was meant for.

One of the best things that happened to me in Canada was in the tiny portage shop of Camp Wapomeo. My cabin-mates were going into a huddle inside. What could be up, I wondered? When they came out they presented me with a real local lumberjack shirt that they'd clubbed together to buy. I'd had a problem with only one pair of shorts and one T-shirt for the summer (we washed them in the lake). Bless you, cabin-mates: you're not forgotten. This must be why I still always have one or two of these shirts around. Why shouldn't an old lady dress like a lumberjack?

It was very, very cold, that lake. Before breakfast we washed in it and then were inspected naked by a camp counsellor – in case, I suppose, of infectious disease. Then, dressed, we paddled canoes across the water to our meeting-point on the other side of the lake (I became a skilled canoeist out there), and together recited a 'Salutation to the Dawn.' This was rather nice. 'For yesterday is only a memory, and tomorrow is only a dream, but today well spent...?' I've forgotten the right words, but not the early morning mist, the smell of coffee, the message of that recitation.

Now that I find the sea off Cornwall far too cold to swim in, I am amazed at how cheerfully we jumped into that clear and icy water. Leeches were its only drawback: fond of warm blood, they clung to our legs and arms. A tin of salt was was kept near, and on getting out we had to shake it over them to get them to curl up and drop, poor things. The only other time I've encountered such leeches was in Nepal, splashing through deep grass. They made for the ankles like fleas.

THE LONG VACATION

The best times at Camp Wapomeo were the canoe trips. As I recall, there would be three or more canoes loaded up with tent and sleeping bags, and some basic foods. A kettle, a frying-pan. Matches of course: we didn't have to drill two sticks in true Baden-Powell fashion. Half a dozen of us, with someone knowledgeable from the camp staff, set off for a few days. There would be hours of paddling (in proper Canadian canoes, of course) and then, probably, some heavy work carrying everything over a portage and repacking the canoes.

The tents we set up were not the cute blow-up things of today: they involved tent-pegs (hard to hammer) and guy-ropes (easy to fall over). Tough stuff. We ate around the camp fire and washed up in the lake. Did I sleep peacefully under that clear starry sky? Probably not: rustling sounds started a rumour that a bear had been trying to get at our stores overnight, or was it a moose? Something northern and exciting, anyway.

Back at camp, there was sailing as well as canoeing, and riding my horse for the season, Comanche, an accommodating creature. I spent some time in the craft workshop. Here I wove a North American style rag rug, to be sent home to England. My mother had sent out a length of Liberty fabric for me from her clothes ration. I had no money for presents to send, but the rag rug went off and survived dangerous seas.

Presents, presents. The year before I left for Canada, I had crept out to buy a little Christmas tree for my parents, hidden it in the potting shed, painted it white and silver, and hung it with presents. For my father, there would have been the usual packet of pipe-cleaners in all colours. I always bought him that for Christmas.

* * * *

From the lake, back to the city. Autumn, winter: snow fell and fell. (Was it falling on those deserted northern lakes?) Spring at last: within days snow had melted everywhere in great gushes. Water ran down our front path, torrented down our hill. Everywhere the forgotten colour green reappeared.

It was about this time that I was confirmed into the Christian faith. Confirmed, in a way... We were all in for it, all our class except Catholics and Jews – Joan too, I think. It was before she and her mother converted to Catholicism. Confirmation at our local church was a question of having a white dress. White shoes to match and nylons, of course: no bobby-sox or black school stockings. I had, from somewhere, the dress, rather floppy and tied in a sash at the back; the shoes, though, were the problem. I had been given white-and-navy peep-toe pumps, but they were too big, and my toes not long enough to peep. Out of an old nylon stocking I made two little round bundles that I pushed through to the end of each shoe. The fear was that they would fall out on my way to the altar.

The Lord was kind and they didn't. I had resolved to take a big gulp of the Communion wine to see if it tasted of blood, or did anything magical to me. It tasted sour, as wine has always tasted to me since. I was confirmed, but into atheism. All the same, what a temptingly primitive, cannibalistic rite the Holy Communion is! I envy true believers.

Adolescence was now approaching or rather, North American teenagery. There was teenage uniform ('Sloppy Joe' sweater, brown and white saddle shoes), teenage rituals (knowing who was top of the Hit Parade each week, listening to the original radio soap operas – *Stella Dallas*, *Life Can Be Beautiful*, *The Shadow Knows* – advertising soap flakes.)

There was the possibility of a bra and lipstick. Our family maidservant, Muriel, had just come back from a honeymoon with her soldier, and Joan and I plied her with questions. We'd seen, of course, the agony aunt's calm words in the women's magazines, but they were... rather insubstantial. Poor Muriel! Whatever we did learn about marriage from her may not have been profitable: I was to become a divorcee, and my foster-sister I think, only avoided the same thing because of her Catholicism.

It was 1943, I was fifteen and been away for three years. How did the possibility of returning home first arise? Most of the Canadian evacuees stayed at least four years. I have one of the great memory-snowdrifts here. What was said? When decided? How were arrangements made? What was paid, and to whom? Was my foster family particularly keen to see me go? Was I quite aware, even, of the arrangements and payments? I longed to go, even though I had such difficulty remembering Oxford. So it was organised: I would be able to take a Portuguese vessel – which was neutral, of course – to Europe, and then get further transport to England. First I was to spend a

THE LONG VACATION

summer holiday with the kind Rhodes friends in Princeton where I had stayed once before, with the twins.

At the US/Canada border there were rough moments, I remember: I was fingerprinted for the first (and only) time, and my girlish clothes (pink spotted skirt, skinny bathing-suit) were tumbled about by Customs officers and left for me to indignantly re-pack. Did I, then, look like an adult, not a child? Which was I?

In Princeton, where on my other visit I had for the first time seen avenues of magnolias in flower, it was the full-on long hot American summer. My hosts' house was one of those white clapboard houses that are the glory of American suburbs. Down a long straight path to the Institute of Advanced Study, Einstein could sometimes be seen shuffling gently about, distinguished by his wearing of sandals with no socks and, of course, by the wild white hair. The socklessness seemed to amaze Americans, though one might think that socks underneath hot-weather sandals took away their point. I wore very clean white socks myself, for I was by now a fully-fledged bobby-soxer. And a fan of Frank Sinatra, which I still remain. I brought his very earliest records back to England in my trunk unchipped, and was remorselessly derided by my parents for it – a 'crooner'! (If only I still had those records: he was never so good again, nor so innocent and sweet-faced.)

I sank into a gentle torpor that summer. My hostess worried that she didn't have entertainment or young companions to offer. No matter. She got me a chameleon (they really do change colour), and in the sitting-room there was one whole wall of American detective stories. I read them all, at an average rate of one and a half per day. I was in suspension.

Daily, vegetables came in fresh from the garden – my first sight of corn on the cob. At night, the garden was full of fireflies. The house dog, an enormous Great Dane, found his way into the dining-room one day and stripped a meal of cold meats with one sweep of his tongue. Down the road, Einstein, I am sure, was still unaware of physicists frantically working towards a coming explosion. '*Oh weh!*', was his cry when he heard the news of the first nuclear explosion.

My host in Princeton was a Quaker, my hostess Christian Scientist: I went on alternate Sundays to Meeting House and to the Church of Christ Scientist (a curious image, Jesus in the laboratory with halo and microscope). I preferred Meeting House, where people were called 'Thee' and there was a lot of silence. Christian Science meant reading out a passage from the Bible, and then its translation, into less comprehensible words, by the mysterious Mrs Eddy.

News of a passage would be given with only 24 hours notice of embarkation. My hostess had already taken me to New York to buy me a Sloppy Joe sweater, a Teddy-bear coat and a pair of saddle shoes – almost the first clothes I had had for a long time that were not from refugee parcels. I didn't see New York again until 1978, but it would appear in my dreams from time to time, always as a place of generosity and pleasure. This was especially connected with the magic of the Automat café, or Horn and Hardart, where dishes were ranged in transparent compartments and could be obtained by putting in dimes and nickels.

THE LONG VACATION

(Why did the Automats disappear? Devaluation of metal coins, perhaps.) We went on waiting for news.

THE LONG VACATION

THE LONG VACATION

1. *Myself with Jim*

THE LONG VACATION

2. *Unhappy in Granny's house in Park Town*

THE LONG VACATION

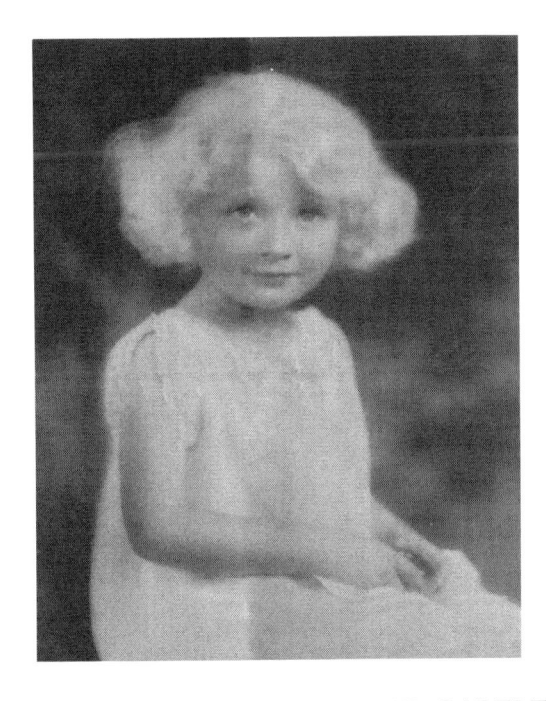

3. *The Scribe:* THE DAUGHTER OF MR CARELTON KEMP ALLEN M.C., THE DISTINGUISHED WARDEN OF RHODES HOUSE, OXFORD: MISS ROSEMARY ALLEN.

Miss Rosemary Allen is the first daughter of Mr. and Mrs. Carleton Kemp Allen. Mr. Allen, who was formerly Professor of Jurisprudence at Oxford, was recently appointed Warden of Rhodes House, Oxford. He is the younger son of the late Rev. William Allen, of Sydney, Australia, and was educated at Newington College, Sydney, the University of Sydney, and New College, Oxford. During the war he served with the Middlesex Regiment, and was Captain and Adjutant. He was twice wounded, and was decorated with the M.C. He was called to the Bar in 1919, and was appointed Professor of Jurisprudence at Oxford in 1929. [PORTRAIT – STUDY BY MARCUS ADAMS]

THE LONG VACATION

4. In Rhodes House garden (1931)

5. My father, C.K. Allen, and myself (1934)

6. *My father in his study*

7. *Lord Lothian*

THE LONG VACATION

8. Mother and father ready to go out

9. Mother preparing for a dinner party

10. The Queen's sister visits Oxford during the 1950s

THE LONG VACATION

11. An Oxford picnic with the Micheners, who were to be my foster parents during the war (1938)

12. Digging up the tennis court for cabbages (1940)

13. The static water tank installed for fear of fire during bombing raids

THE LONG VACATION

14. Norah and Roland Michener, my foster parents during the war

15. 'I'm going on an adventure!'

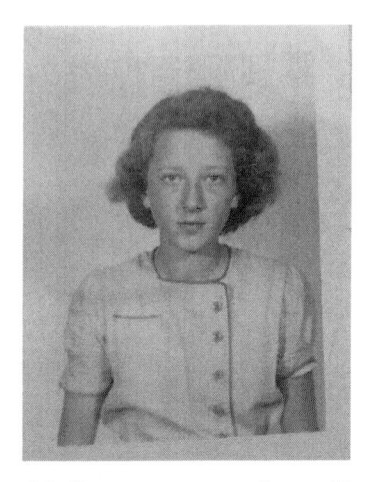

16. 'I want to go to home!'

THE LONG VACATION

17. The 'Bermondsey Boys'

18. My sons in the park

19. Simon and Mark Dinnage

20. Donald Winnicott

THE LONG VACATION

21. Receiving an award for journalism from Iris Murdoch

22. My cottage in Abergavenny. From a painting by Trevor Pether

23. Nelson Mandela with students of the Mandela Rhodes Foundation (2010)

THE LONG VACATION

3. *And coming back*

THE LONG VACATION

The day came.

Few letters from those days have survived, but in front of me I have one from my Princeton host to my father.

'I received a long distance telephone message yesterday', he writes,

> at 12:25 yesterday that Rosemary's visa had at last been authorized, that she would have to appear in person to apply for it in New York before three o'clock, and that her ship would sail from Philadelphia today at twelve. I dashed over to the house, had the luck to get Rosemary to New York for Cook's, the Portuguese and British Consulates, and the American income tax authorities. We returned in time for dinner with all the formalities completed, finished Rosemary's packing in the evening, and she and Marie left for Philadelphia at nine this morning.
>
> Naturally, Rosemary is in a state of wild excitement about returning to England, and I am sure she will enjoy every minute of the voyage unless she is seasick. Indeed, she was a little disappointed to learn that children travelling alone are given priorities on the trip by plane from Lisbon to England. I think she would like to stay in Lisbon six weeks [as I did] and see some of the spies she has read about.

'I should like to be present when you set eyes on her after three years', he adds slyly. 'I expect that you will be amazed. I shall be particularly interested to know what you think of her accent.' My accent, oh my accent! So all-important to English people. It was by now, of course, purest Canadian. I found the English stuffy way of speaking pretty comical.

So I was there the next day, at the docks in Philadelphia. It was a bright morning: the memory is one of those that can be treasured and burnished up like old silver over the years. The scintilla of light on black depths, the slap of water against wood as we searched quay after quay, the spelling-out, eventually, of letters on the bow of a ship – *Nyassa*.

There was no seasickness or house-high wave, on that return journey. Innocent *Nyassa* was fully lit up too, trusting to her neutrality for safety.

There were, though, smells, extraordinarily pungent ones. The cabin that I shared with three other teenage evacuees trying to get back to England was placed precisely between the lavatories and the galley. Smells of stale oil and burned potato mingled with faecal overkill from the flooded toilets. The upper berth on the corridor side of the cabin was especially to be avoided because things crawled in through the ventilator and onto the blankets. By things I don't mean just large seagoing beetles: these were almost crab-sized. Whiskered too, I think.

Then one day, suddenly, we anchored, and a mass, a rout of Portuguese airmen began to board the ship. We were at Terceira, third of Portugal's Azores islands and nearly halfway between the States and Lisbon. These islands are not much visited by tourists, though I believe Princess Diana holidayed there. We rootless and rather dazed girls, glad to be away from geography lessons, were not as much interested in the islands as in the dark-eyed young men that overran the ship. There seemed to be no accommodation for them: they bedded down in every corner of the deck. From below closed portholes, romantic serenades floated up.

The islands, I now realise, were of great interest to both the Allies and the Axis powers as military bases. As early as 1941 there had been discussions about them, impetuous Americans being dissuaded from invading by the more diplomatic British. Salazar, Portugal's dictator for so long, was treading a tightrope during these years of neutrality. During the Spanish Civil War he had naturally inclined towards Franco, and took in a flood of Spanish refugees. Perhaps he had inclined towards Hitler earlier in the war; or perhaps the centuries-old alliance between Portugal and England did stand for something. He had a Nazi invasion through Spain to fear, as well as Bolsheviks in the east. By 1943, in any case, the Allies were the team to back, and it all got very friendly. The oddest thing I found in tracing this period was that, during it, a delegation of Oxford dons went out to Coimbra to bestow an honorary degree on Salazar. What was that about? Softening him up?

While I was waiting through that Princeton summer, Azores negotiations must have been fast and furious. Access was at first granted just in principle; I like Churchill's comment on that, in private communication: 'The great thing is to worm our way in and then, without raising any principles, swell ourselves out.'

And so they did, swelled themselves out like billy-o. Terceira became a base for both the Portuguese and American Air Forces. From autumn 1943, Atlantic convoys would be safer from U-boats and could follow a better route than the dangerous one on which we evacuee children were sent out, some to their deaths.

Why the handsome airmen were sent to Estoril (a resort near Lisbon), as the English passengers were, I don't know. Certainly they were there: I have a photo of two of them sitting by a sea-front palm tree. On board *Nyassa* we danced with them in the evenings, using French as a common language. Because I wore my trousers rolled up in the 1940s fashion, I was called '*la pêcheuse*' In Estoril they taught us Portuguese songs and folk dances. When later I was teaching myself Italian, I was convinced it was pronounced as Portuguese.

I didn't go back to Estoril until fifty years later. It didn't occur to me to do so. Then, after a holiday with my friends in the Minho of northern Portugal, I went to Lisbon on my own for a couple of days and took a little electric train to Estoril. Under prickly pines in the small park, I mooned around and read *In Memoriam*. Things were in place just as I remembered: the Parque Hotel (where I stayed) on one side, the Palaçio Hotel on the other, the casino in between. This was no overdeveloped Torremolinos but a stately and long-established resort for rich Lisbonians. *The Rough Guide to Portugal* describes it as pretentious, studded with grandiose expatriate villas (Spanish? German?). No haven for backpackers, certainly; but in 1943 a haven for just about everybody from both sides in the war – refugees, politicians, gamblers, aristos. It was two months before this that Rose Macaulay had visited Lisbon for the *Spectator* (a result, no doubt, of our new, cuddly relationship with the Azores owners). At a cosmopolitan dinner party, she writes, the Portuguese host would tell the servants: 'The

English are coming; we must put away Adolf and Benito. And some of the French, so we won't have the old Maréchal. But Francisco can stay: I have no Spanish tonight.'

There must have been spies in Estoril, but how to know? I think, too, there must have been officers in German uniform among the crowds that went to the casino every night. How much a better story if I could remember them! As it is, I remember dusty sand, a performing monkey, schoolgirl talks laced with panic about meeting our families again, and a fellow guest pouring olive oil (for cleaning ears, surely?) all over his plate like gravy.

So the airmen who charmed us on board ship were, I imagine, being brought back to make room for Allied installations; the hitch that kept us English passengers waiting in luxury in Estoril for several weeks must have been to do with the final negotiations that let Allied forces land on Terceira in October. (Could there have been haggling, as in: 'Not another week, unless we can bring the English passengers back'; 'Only if we keep the north shore'?) In any case, the autumn sun, the dry beach, the faded luxury of the Parque were a kind of nervous heaven, time ticking by too fast and yet resisted: perhaps we should rather drift on here than meet the culture shock of wartime Britain, and our half-remembered families?

Marian had been, uneasily, with her Jewish relatives in Brooklyn and was going back to Willesden, a place I hadn't heard of; Betty and Audrey were returning to Birmingham. Betty, almost old enough to get into the army, was being seriously courted by one of the airmen. While we looked out across the sea one day, she said: 'I wonder if we'll all ever meet again.' I could only freeze. I have never been able to talk about partings or reunions. We knew we were going to miss one another. (We didn't meet again, but for a while exchanged letters about the strange experiences of England.)

I don't know where I was when the news came through of an immediate flight to London. There was quick packing, goodbyes (we were not all to go on the same plane), a bus into Lisbon, take-off from the river Tagus. Then I am sitting on the floor of a blacked-out bitterly cold seaplane[10] – a Sunderland, I believe it was called. From the lack of seats and heating it must have been used for troop movements. Though my friends were not on this plane, I did have a companion of a sort with me: he was in my coat pocket – a small quiet rabbit called Antonio Pinto. Just before I left, I had heard that someone on the beach at neighbouring Cascais was selling a litter of baby rabbits, and a friend had brought me back one.

I wanted, I suppose, something remaining from the weeks in Portugal, something warm to stay with me. Antonio stayed patiently still through Customs and inspections, and never peed in my pocket.

From Lisbon to England was quite a long flight, a good many shivery hours. I hadn't, of course, ever been in the air before, and wasn't to be again until 1950. We stopped briefly in Ireland, I suppose to refuel; through a crack in the blinds I could see thatched, white cottages and thought, 'So – Ireland does look like the pictures'.

---

[10] A seaplane was a craft that came down on water, not land. I don't know if they still exist.

It was in Poole harbour on the south coast that we finally came down. A boat trip ashore, an arrival at Poole railway station, have been censored out. Next, I am at Victoria station in the blackout, fearful of not recognising my father. A friend of mine, who came back later, told me she burst into tears when she saw that it was a decrepit-seeming old man who was looking for her. Somehow my father and I found each other in the dark. He took me to a restaurant nearby – some were open for business without ration cards – and I had to tell him about my Portuguese rabbit. He was puzzled; but an attendant in the ladies' cloakroom helped me put Antonio in a drawer with some scraps of food.

And so to Oxford, the home I had lost, and was partly to find again.

For the first few days I kept falling asleep. It was the Thames Valley damp climate, I was told. Rhodes House was big, enormous. My mother excitedly took me round, introducing me to servants and secretaries. She expected me to remember everything, but of course I didn't. She had had a pink dressing-gown made for me out of some curtain material. We put my rabbit in a stone-floored lobby, with some water and lettuce. In this picture, my twelve-year-old brother seems to be missing. Was he already away at boarding school? It was autumn, around school time.

I dread finishing the rabbit story; but I must. My mother told me the next day that, sadly, he had knocked a cushion over on himself in the night and suffocated. Of course this was impossible, but at the time I believed it. I didn't cry – it had always been forbidden – but when I think of my rabbit, so brave and trusty, dying so far away from home, the pain is terrible.

* * * *

Being 'home' again was, in a nervous way, happy. I knew that my teenage spots were awful and had to be submitted to a doctor; I knew that once again I had an accent that set everyone's nerves on edge: I knew that my way of walking, even, was wrong (I was shown how I must take longer, slower, more English steps). And, drying dishes. I must hold the towel in a different way. 'No. like *this*.'

On my mother's desk, soon after I got back, were three letters to people laid out very visibly: all were much the same, and had the same sentence in it – something like 'Rosemary is not so... was it 'haughty'?, 'tiresome'?, 'odd'? as she was when she arrived'. This hurt.

All the same, I wasn't a foreigner any more: not a cuckoo in an already occupied nest. Perhaps I hadn't been so much of a cuckoo. Try as I will to be clear, memory pushes facts about. When I won a scholarship to university, my foster-mother wrote to say how proud she was of me, how she boasted about me to her friends. (The product, myself, was satisfactory at that moment, but both mothers wanted the credit.) She thanked me for the present of a book – 'You know my tastes by now and it pleases me that you do.'

Can she, she asks, send me a paper pattern for dressmaking, a fountain pen, a beret to replace the straw hat that wouldn't fit into my trunk? But though she signs herself 'Aunt Norah', she reproaches me for never having called her that: 'Surely I had some name in your mind?' It's true, and I am ashamed; I managed, somehow, never to allow her a name. I suppose I felt that as I had my own Aunt Anne and Aunt Edith... But it's not excusable.

Gradually, I was getting used to this new, or not-so-new place. Letters came from my Portugal friends. Using the notepaper of the Companhia Nacional de Navegação, Marian writes that she is waiting to be assigned work. *Nyassa* is now taking refugees to Palestine. Why do English girls wear their skirts so droopy? And am I getting the hang of the English accent? She's met a nice RAF boy. My letter was 'a refreshing gust of wind', she said, bringing back our times in Estoril – the hot chocolate at the *sala de chai*, movies at the Old Casino – and we must write to each other once a week. Betty wrote too: she has just been to Leslie Howard's final film – am I still crazy about him? (Oh, yes, Betty. Still.) Except when she gets letters from Canada, she writes, 'the whole experience (being evacuated) seems rather like a dream. Do you ever feel that?'

Did I? Do I? Perhaps. But things went along fairly smoothly, though I knew everything un-English about me was obnoxious and must be scrubbed out. Smoothly, but it was like walking on ice that has ominous dark patches.

There were things missing. Of course the dolls' house had had to be thrown out, but where was the Dead Sea apple that Aunt Edith had brought me back from her holiday? The tangled seed pearls that my godfather had given me? My collection of blue china cats? Still, the rag rug that I had sent from far-off camp was triumphantly there, and even the mat that I had embroidered in cross-stitch in kindergarten.

Other things were there that never had been when I left – in particular, substitute daughters. Some of the London evacuees had returned for a while: one in particular had been so wonderful that she had brought my mother breakfast in bed. I heard a lot about her.

Rhodes House was astonishingly sociable then – not, I think, with Rhodes Scholars (it was hard to tell) but with servicemen and all kinds of overseas visitors. In the Hall named after Rhodes's wily friend Milner, dances were held for servicemen to the music of Joe Loss on gramophone. The Polish airmen, suave favourites of us girls (they kissed our hands!) brought music for folk-dancing, and we learned the *krakowiak* and the old-fashioned waltz. A Norwegian au-pair, sobbing over her lover, lived in, and a new schoolgirl evacuee. People would drop in for tea. This was set out on a lace cloth in the sitting-room, and was the one meal where we were allowed to bring down our books to read in armchairs, while the cook's cat might come in from the kitchen to stretch out in front of a log fire. Lights were low. In spite of rationing, there would always be something staunchly English for tea – sandwiches and perhaps a cake, got by queuing at the Oliver and Gurden factory in north Oxford. Tea was a meal, just as much as supper. Then the doorbell might ring, we would put away our books, summon up smiles and Miss Fischer the refugee artist might sweep ebulliently in, ignorant of the niceties of English teatime.

Although I had eaten luxuriously in Canada, shortages in Britain caused me no great distress. Potatoes were never rationed, and bread only occasionally. There were turnips, and stewed apples, and suchlike gloomy things. Our ration cards, put together, produced a roast every Sunday, and afterwards there would be a bowl of dripping, for heavenly dripping toast. But by winter it was cold – oh, so cold. Rhodes House had central heating of a sort, but in wartime it scarcely functioned. I had never had chilblains on my fingers before, nor needed two heated water bottles to pre-heat icy sheets. In classrooms in Canada there had always been a thermometer to check the temperature of 70 degrees; what the temperatures were in Oxford schoolrooms and corridors and bathrooms I can hardly imagine. Glumly, I went into Chilprufe under-vests.

But school, Oxford High again, was the very opposite of my Toronto one. There I had been invisible, non-existent: not bullied, not noticed, a child among gigantic, sexy teenagers. Back at school from abroad, to my surprise I found myself a rather glamorous figure. I had been on an aeroplane! I had an accent like people in the movies (known as the flicks): I was rumoured to have some nylons. A group of classmates cornered me one day. 'Could we ask you something?' 'Sure.' 'Do you wear a brassiere?' 'Sure I do!' My Canadian foster-mother had taken me to be specially measured for one. Eyes wide, the girls pondered the information.

I was a bit of a heroine.

This was good. But as my teens progressed, the difficulty between my mother and myself, that would later escalate, was already growing. When my cat, in later life, had a kitten returned to her after its stay at the vet, she was doubtful about it. She sniffed around it with distaste: it smelled rather clean, not kitteny enough. My mother had sent off one parcel, a child in socks, and got back a different one, in bra and one-inch heels.

Teenagers of course are expected to be difficult nowadays. Not so in the 1940s. My crimes were not drug-taking, staying out all night, playing pop music very loud (only, very softly, Sinatra to remind me of where I'd come from). Sometimes I wasn't up early (that meant bedclothes brusquely stripped off me). Sometimes I arrived late at that peaceful tea-table. Sometimes I was sent out on my bicycle to queue for something and came back with the wrong thing, not quite understanding the idiom.

Or perhaps I was indeed awful? A friend who was evacuated for even longer than me is sure that she put her parents through hell when she got back. My brother tells me I used to lock my bedroom door – so shocking! There was, of course, a huge house to clean, and a much reduced staff: girls who used to go into domestic service had been directed into armaments factories or the Forces. A situation developed where I wouldn't offer to do the work unless I was asked, and wouldn't get asked unless I offered. 'How weird', said a better-behaved friend in amazement. It was weird. And of importance only because the weirdness worsened, and was never resolved.

My clothes might be wrong. I remember coming downstairs for the weekly dance in a dress to which I had

THE LONG VACATION

just put the last stitches with the sewing-machine from Park Town. It was dark blue and rather woolly, and so perhaps not the right thing for a dance. But I had *just* finished it! And pinned on to it a white imitation gardenia.[11] But there was a great fuss, a tremendous fuss: I could not, clearly go in like that. I did, of course – dumb defiance was my stance – but was miserable all evening. How sad that, when I have forgotten so much, I should in my old age remember this so sharply.

Reading could be a battleground, even. It has always been an addiction for me, a life-saving one. Around the end of school days I started a few pages of a diary, and I see that I was reading *Candide*, Hoffmannsthal, the *Odyssey*, Traherne, *Zuleika Dobson*, Whitman, C. S. Lewis, the *Goncourt Diaries*, Bacon, *Sons and Lovers*[12]. Not bad for a sixteen-year-old. But seeing me sitting with a book was sometimes an exasperation: windows would be flung open – 'so stuffy in here' – and I would be sent off on the bicycle. When I won my scholarship I was rushed round the building to tell blank-faced housemaids and secretaries the thrilling news – but how do you pass exams if not by reading a lot of books?

'Should literature be a criticism of life or a reflection of it?' was the kind of question I was asking myself in that schoolgirl diary – thinking, no doubt, of exam questions to

---

[11] These fake flowers, painted with some sort of luminous substance so as to glow in the dark, were sold for wearing in the blackout. So if you went outside with one pinned roguishly on – unlikely, really – you would not be run over.

[12] Also I see 'De Quincey on Virgil's cow'. What could this be?

126

come. '*L'écueil particulier du genre romantique c'est le faux*', I copy faithfully from Sainte-Beuve. 'Langland and Kafka as religious allegory', I suggest. 'Are there such things as absolute values?' Oh dear. But there are also mentions of parties: ('moderate fun'), trying to learn poker ('won 1/11d.'), entertainment ('listened to Brains Trust'), duty ('mended stockings'). There are meetings and visits with mysterious beings known only as A. and W. and P. (There were aspects of these encounters that didn't get written). Giggling is mentioned, and the meat queue at Aldens, and curling my hair. 'Dull Rhodes Scholar to lunch', sadly. A birthday arrives ('flowers from P. (!)') and *The Rivals* at the Oxford Playhouse. Much skating on the frozen floods of Port Meadow, sometimes with the boys from Radley School: fiery sunsets over Wytham Hill, an icy wind. A lot of sore throats and colds are mentioned: were we all rather undernourished? A visit to London to find a pair of shoes with my coupons, seeing as usual the black, decaying backs of London houses when the train was near Paddington. No possible shoes anywhere.

As to be expected from an adolescent, there is much in the diary about WHO AM I? 'My personality becomes more and more elusive, goes away terrifyingly, leaving nothing but fear' – and so on. Even compared with others of that age, I was beset and confused, a potential analysand already. The longing to be looked at to be sure I existed. The falling-into space when someone left me... One sentence there I don't laugh at, because it sums up something I have felt again and again: 'If only for one moment, one could sweep out all the ideas of books and people, and think for a little while absolutely clearly and

THE LONG VACATION

originally – I feel that if I could get down to that clear and original, though minute, spark, I would know what I am.'

* * * *

VE Day. 1945: The war in Europe truly over. (The Japanese war, to end on VJ Day, meant much less in Britain). Our evacuee, Anne, and I were in trouble, but it was worth it.

We knew that there were celebrations in town. After the dark years, lights were brilliantly on: from Carfax drifted faint sounds of music. We didn't stop for permission to go out – but how could we stay in? Right along the High Street and under Magdalen Tower, lit up and bright against the night sky was where the crowd were thickest – dancing, singing, shouting, in a way I'd never seen before. People always say, 'we were going wild', my historian son said to me recently, rather bored. Well, damn it: we were. 'This is the most historic moment of my life', I told myself solemnly.

When we crept home we found – oh, horror! – that we had been locked out. Not as punishment, but just on the assumption that girls wouldn't be out that late. We went to our neighbour next door, who kept late hours, and she gave us beds for the night. She promised faithfully not to tell the parents – but she did, the treacherous creature. Anne and I got a talking-to, but not a very severe one. It's a pity that my parents never saw that scene for themselves.

VE Day: and I go back to wondering how much I, and my schoolmates, had really followed or understood the war news. Hitler, and what Churchill called the 'Narzees' (thus showing his contempt) could be treated as comical: 'Run Adolf, run, run, run', people sang: 'We will knock the stuffing out of you, / Old fat-guts Goering and Goebbels too...'. That was propaganda: keep morale up by pretending our toxic enemies are just foreign silly-billies. Certainly – unless I have a complete memory block – when I pressed to come home in 1943 I had no thought of it as going into danger. Nor did my friends in Estoril. Real danger time seemed to be over, the war moving towards an assured ending. And yet the Vl and V2 unmanned rockets ('doodlebugs' or 'buzz bombs') that smashed into London a year after I got back showed that the enemy could still put up a fight. This offensive was called considered a revenge action and we ourselves, of course, had massively bombed German cities such as Dresden. How massively was not quite realised; the thinking, I believe, was just that they bombed us, we bombed them... .

Of Communist Russia little was really known by us ordinary people. When I read how Stalin caused more innocent deaths and suffering than Hitler, it still gives me a shock. Russia was our gallant ally, no? Scarves and gloves were knitted for freezing soldiers on the eastern front; 'Uncle Joe', sat orientally grinning between Churchill and Roosevelt in photographs. Russian soldiers were indeed freezing and dying, though it was hardly grasped how many; and Russia was certainly our ally. Left-leaning people such as myself went on believing in Russia – vaguely – far too long, though I learned something from

THE LONG VACATION

the Polish airmen we danced with. Denigration of the Soviet Union, it was felt, came from the elderly and the right-wing. For me, it took many years and the reading of well-researched books to be able to grasp the full history of our wartime ally.

VJ Day, I have said, did not mean nearly as much as that first great celebration. And yet the seriousness of the two atomic bomb strikes on Japan did get through. There must have been photographs of the unutterable desolation of the destroyed cities, and there was some idea, already, that the use of this ultimate weapon had been a terrible step. Defenders argued that many lives in the fighting forces had been saved by cutting the war short. Fear of atomic attack, of course, went on and on. 'Naturally there'll be another atomic bomb', my father said in the 1950s. 'But I won't be here to see it.' No, but I will, and my children, I thought. Thanks.

Oxford. The teenage life that, blindly and quite pleasantly, trundled on. Twice a day the one remaining parlourmaid gently banged the gong for meals. Often I was late for them. There was displeasure. If it was a question of lateness for breakfast, there was a chorus of 'Good evening'. Giggling and dancing went on, and intensive scholarly reading, and little connection between the two. To be a divided person was what I was accustomed to. Rationing went on and on, and I stood in many queues. I cycled to Elliston's lending library to exchange my mother's books: 'Something similar to the last one, please'. My brother practised the piano, more and more brilliantly.

My father was mainly in his study. Dreadfully boring Rhodes persons came and went. I went to a sermon in the university church by the distinguished scholar and Christian apologist C. S. Lewis, now more known for his wonderful fairytales. 'No need to write about it'; I scribbled down; 'I'll never forget it.' I have forgotten it. Or have I? Wasn't it something about hell being forever estranged from God? Perhaps he had been reading about Belsen.

For some reason, my parents always sniggered when Lewis's name was mentioned. I can't think why; he was the most brilliant lecturer of the time, and not thought to be 'homo' or anything dreadful like that. Teasing was much favoured in the family, perhaps for a wrong pronunciation or a waving-about of hands while talking. They should, of course, stay still in the lap; foreigners waved them about. 'I expect you think you're misunderstood by your parents', my father quipped, 'teasingly'. I certainly did.

Though this was a university family, there were phrases around the dining table that expressed disapproval, not just of excitable foreigners, but of intellectualism. 'Clever-clever' was one and there was 'affected', 'arty' and (firmly, from my mother) *rather unnecessary*'. Our near neighbour Maurice Bowra, Warden of Wadham, may have fallen into the unnecessary category: I understand he was famous for his naughty wit. The word 'Bloomsbury' I assumed to be the very synonym of artiness and affectedness.

Politically my father was more deeply conservative than you might expect an Australian to be, and was in a torment of exasperation with the postwar Labour government. Around this time he brought out a small book, printed on wartime paper, on civil liberties (*Democracy and the Individual*). I remember an outraged shout over the *Observer* one Sunday: 'It's been reviewed by a Communist!' The reviewer was in fact George Orwell, far from a Communist – though he did, admittedly, bring the name of Marx twice into his review. The author's extensive and able enquiry into the working of democracy is all very well, wrote Orwell, but he ignores the sheer fact of economic inequality. That fact means that Britain is not a democracy: 'It is a plutocracy haunted by the ghost of a caste system,' Splendid: Orwell's style is so excellent that I cannot resist quoting another part of his review:

> Marxism may be a mistaken theory but it is a useful instrument for testing other systems of thought, rather like one of those long-handled hammers with which they tap the wheels of locomotives. Tap! Is this wheel cracked? Tap! Is this writer a bourgeois?... It is surprising how often a pretentious book will seem suddenly hollow if you apply to it the simple question: Does this writer, or does he not, take account of the economic basis of society?

The idea of my father as a steam train having his wheels tapped by a Marxist railwayman[13] is rather charming.

Orwell's point seemed to me perfectly clear and perfectly valid. It still does.

One small attempt to bridge economic inequality was perhaps the annual Oxford visit of the 'Bermondsey boys'. Bermondsey was then a very deprived area, where families could scarcely afford holidays, and a group of boys were

---

[13] Perhaps a sinister Russian peasant muttering, '*Il faute battre*' as in *Anna Karenina*?

THE LONG VACATION

brought down[14] by some charity for a break. Or for them to see how the other half – no, the other very small fraction – lived. What did they think of us, I wonder? Were they awed by the toffs? I doubt it. They were no doubt shown round, given a game of football, enjoyed a bit of fun. Around my own age as they were on these visits, some may be alive now, and I wish I knew what they remember. Rhodes House's main contribution was providing sandwiches and doing a lot of washing-up. 'This water is terribly greasy', I said; but nobody took any notice. It was only for the Bermondsey boys.

My 'war work' if the war went on long enough, I had decided, would be as a Land Girl (farming) or a VAD (nursing assistant). I wasn't keen on wearing scratchy khaki or sleeping in a Nissan hut, but Land Girls wore attractively butch corduroy breeches, and VADs snowy white aprons. The war of course was soon to end, but we schoolgirls did contribute. One of my jobs was to assist at a blood donor clinic, for which I did at least have the snowy apron, and a red cross on my chest. I was not entrusted with even the very simple job of checking the haemoglobin level in blood samples: my responsibility was to see that each donor had a cup of tea before leaving the clinic – to ensure, I suppose, that their veins filled up a bit so that they would not collapse, emptied out, in the street. I did once forget the cup of tea, but never found out the sequel. Another year there was a call for postal workers. The choice was between the sorting office and doing the deliveries, and I had the happy job of postwoman for the

---

[14] If they had come to join a college, they would have been going *up* to Oxford.

school holidays. Mail was then delivered even on Christmas Day, so as well as being able to miss church I was welcomed in to have mince pies (wartime recipe) and hot drinks. I think I did a better job than present-day postmen.

And there were the farm camps, heavy vacation work organised to help out farms where young men had gone into the Forces. It wasn't a question of petting ponies or scratching pigs' backs: lifting potatoes was a dull day-long job. We slept in army tents, the round ones with all feet angled to the centre. My sleeping-bag was old and flimsy, but straw palliasses were provided to lay under them. On the whole it was fun, a change from books, books, books. A different farm stay was rather spoiled by embarrassment. My mother, obsessed by my pallor and her belief in fresh air, had arranged it without telling me, and nobody seemed to be expecting me. It was the home farm of some extremely grand estate. I was working alongside girls of the débutante class, girls who murmured that Lady So-and-So had come to stay *without a maid!* But they were very kind to me. Our job was getting the harvest in, and this meant forking up the stooks by muscle power, while a partner stood on the cart to catch and stack them. To miss a beat on this assembly line slowed things down badly.

I'm glad I had the chance to know pre-mechanised farming in this simple form. I don't want to know, really, how it's done now.

THE LONG VACATION

(ii)

By now I had left school, rather early. By scraping the bottom of the barrel, the authorities had made me a school prefect, and prefects had to read the lesson at Prayers. This was very frightening; and made more so by being called to the headmistress's study afterwards and told I had not – somehow – done it properly. 'And your mother tells me you don't make your bed in the mornings', she added. So, as I had passed all necessary exams, even the wretched Latin without which one could not be admitted to the university, I left.

For a while it was back to books. Back to some heavy thinking – too much, certainly. I felt the dark gap opening up. I was into Sartre, of course, and all the gloomy Europeans. 'I am an indelible transparency', wrote the founder of existentialism, and I nodded in agreement. Hopkins even, a hundred years before, was speaking for me: 'All things alike, all in the same degree, rebuff me with blank unlikeness'. This was a sensation that often returned in later life. The blankness. *Realness* ebbing away, always being searched for.

I was steeped in Kafka's diaries too, when an amazing thing happened. Looking round a ravaged corner of London for a cheap temporary room, I mentioned to the landlady that I came from Oxford. She was stout, greying, wrapped in a dirty apron. 'Oxford?', she said in a strong

German accent. 'Do you know the Kafka Society?' I didn't, I said, but I was interested, very interested, in Kafka. 'He was my husband', she said.

I was dumbfounded, too dumbfounded to ask questions. Oh why, *why* didn't I? I knew that in the last stages of tuberculosis, the 40-year-old Kafka had lived in Berlin and then a sanatorium with a young girl called Dora Dymant, that her father had forbidden her to marry him because of his age and his illness.

At the end, when he couldn't speak, Kafka jotted down notes. Could he have some icecream, he asked? Who telephoned? He has coughed up so much sputum that he has dreamed he should get a Nobel prize for it. 'Move the lilacs into the sun now.' 'Please be careful that I don't cough in your face.' I didn't even take the room. It wasn't very nice.

I never wanted to go to university. Once when I had been to one of the women's colleges for an extra tutorial in Latin – that accursed language required for almost every course – I had gone past the doors to a Hall where some meal was being served up. There they all were, huddled in rows around the dinner tables. I shuddered: 'Never,' I thought. Just more of school and even more boring. I could read all the books there were on my own without crowding into that dining-room with a coagulation of other schoolgirls.

'I don't want to go to college,' I said to my parents. They changed the subject. What I secretly wanted was to be a housewife, to have an apron and a carpet sweeper, perhaps even a vacuum cleaner. I couldn't cook – we weren't much allowed into the kitchen – but I could surely learn.

But how to get out of going to college? I was, at the time, so stifled by my parents that the only jobs I could literally imagine were their own. Before coming to Rhodes House, my father had been a lawyer. Could I go to college but train as a lawyer? 'Impossible,' he said: 'You have to be very robust to argue cases in the Law Courts'. (In this he was right, and I admit the attraction of the law was partly that there were about 50 men to one girl on the course.) My mother had done a little 'social work'; I suggested I train for that. 'Impossible', she said placidly. 'You have to be unselfish to be a social worker, and you're very selfish'.

So I had to give in, but first I had the gap year.

My stay in Switzerland was a sunny, easy time. In a steep street above Lac Léman, I stayed in Mademoiselle Schmidt's Swiss *pension*, ostensibly to better my French. We were two Czech girls, a Greek count (young, beautiful), a covey of blond boys from Uppsala, a few other English.

Switzerland was war-free, stress-free, abounding in *politesse* and good fresh food. (Asking at the station café for an omelette, I was stunned to be told it had to be a three-egg one.) There was some learning of French, but even more of international friendship and boundary-breaking. 'I was sure that Sweden was the best country in the world', said Tage (the Swedes spoke perfect English): 'I took it for granted. But I see now there *are* other countries.'

I put on red nail polish, went to a nightclub (they played 'Tico-tico'), and smoked a cigarette. I drank three glasses of wine and was sick. The Greek count climbed in my window. Most of the day we spent at the *piscine* turning a smooth bronze – there was no silly fear of sunshine then. We went on the lake in little steamers and danced on deck.

My father, surprisingly, came out for a short holiday. It was recharge-the-batteries time again, but I was delighted to see him and met him at the airport with a bunch of bananas, not seen at home since 1939. In the sun he relaxed a little. We went for lakeside walks, saw a movie starring the suavely sinister Louis Jouvet. We shopped, choosing with care a lace blouse for my mother, but she never wore it.

After we all dispersed I kept in touch with my polyglot friends for a time. Was it Dante who wrote that there is no worse suffering than remembering happy times when they they are over? I don't agree. I'm glad to think there was that simple time of fun, when everyone seemed to like me – it wasn't quite to be repeated. Later on, the dark patches under smooth ice were to shiver.

Leaving home for college meant farewell to the whole Rhodes 'thing': to that scarcely grasped background to my growing up. What a story – all unknown to me – it was! And how glad I am that none of it, not the decisions, meetings, memos, reports, altercations, problems, ideals and compromises, dead ends and solutions, were visited on us two children far up in the nursery wing, or teenaging about downstairs beneath the tense gaze of Rhodes's portrait.

It is only now, though, that I can see how the separations and preoccupations inseparable from the Rhodes buildings and machinery could be an imperfect seed-bed for children. The great dome with marble floor and Greek inscription, the halls, library, lecture rooms, offices, and the undusted metal bookstacks stretching into darkness in the cellars, had been planned with only a small niche for young growing things.

* * * *

I had gained, at 17, my scholarship to Somerville which enabled me – I wanted this at all costs – to live in College rather than at home as my mother wanted. And now I had my bed-sitting room there with its narrow bed and very small electric fire. It was cold, unbelievably cold in these bedrooms, particularly during my first year. The War was over, but as well as continued rationing of food and clothes, heating was severely cut down that winter – wasn't there a strike, a coalminers' strike? We were allowed to have these little heaters on for two hours a day to dry our hair after washing it – our un-coiffed, unsprayed, ungelled, untinted, bouncy hair. (Shampoo was scarce but just obtainable: 'Friday night is Amami night' said the advertisements.) The weekly essay had to be written under a blanket with a hot water bottle.

Being up *at* Oxford rather than living *in* it was not as happy as I'd hoped. Something of Rhodes-ism still hung about me. Any day, at breakfast time, my mother might call to see if I had made my bed. If I saw bedclothes shaken out from my window I hid in a friend's room until the coast was clear. A clique of rather glamorous and cosmopolitan friends gathered and I hovered on the outskirts (some of them are still alive now and good friends). I would hear laughter in the room above and would think of going up there: 'May I join you?', I could have said, but somehow didn't dare. Sometimes I wouldn't even be invited to Ken Tynan's parties. 'Who was he?' asked a young friend helping me with typing. Ken? Actor, writer, theatre critic, and in my time the hub of university social life.

When final examinations approached, I didn't realise that I was expected to get a First. I don't think it occurred to me. I had lent all my Anglo-Saxon notes to a friend of a friend who never returned them in time for my viva (the oral examination that decides your final class). Throughout the one week – I think it was only one week – in which our exams lasted, I believe I actually didn't manage to sleep at all, or very little. I didn't think of asking my parents or a doctor for sleeping pills. Oxford, as you know, is the 'City of Bells' and those bells ring the quarter-past, the half-past, the quarter-to and the hour and I heard them, I believe, almost every night of that week. So when I was told with some sorrow that I had just failed to get a First Class degree I was amazed that I had passed the exams at all.

Had I really learned anything? I read Milton in a way that I would never have read on my own, perhaps. I learned that one must never make a statement about something literary without quoting an example of it. When very much later I became a journalist and book reviewer, I found myself following that rule – the wonderful, or funny, or even awful bits of the work under review seemed so much more worthwhile than anything I could say about them. I have heard, however, that there is something called 'quoter's itch'. I don't think I have actually ever been accused of it.

After these exams, I with a friend of mine, both quite near Firsts, went to the Oxford Appointments Board for advice. We were told not to hope of getting anything highfalutin like jobs at the BBC or a publishing firm. Don't even think of it. Learn shorthand-typing. And so we did. I don't think this could happen today.

We took our shorthand-typing, however, to Paris and got jobs in the typing pool there at UNESCO. It was then in the 16-ième quarter of Paris in an enormous converted hotel which had been the headquarters of the Gestapo during the War. Post-war Paris – this was the place for quaintness and charm, but I have forgotten rather too much of it. We went, I know, to Montmartre where we listened to jazz and guitars and beautiful black singers; on the *quatorze* (14th July) we danced at the *Balle des Pompiers*, grannies and kids and everyone else together. There were, I also remember, very poor people in the streets who looked as if they had only just survived the starvation of the last year of the War. Coffee was hard to get – there were dregs made from ground-up acorns – and once, when I hadn't the rail fare back to England, I auctioned a tin of Nescafé on the platform of Gare du Nord. I got a good price.

I lived in a northern suburb that was mainly Algerian, in a very cold room, at the top of a bleak hotel. If my English boyfriend came to visit me in Paris, he had to be sneaked up past an extremely frightening lady on the ground floor. If I wanted to heat up a glass of wine with some lemon juice, which was an odd thing I did in in order to sleep well, I had to light some rather dangerous fuel in a tiny casket, put a saucepan on it and warm it up for a nightcap.

The Marais district where I stay nowadays when I go to Paris was then a quaint, crooked slum rather than home of boutiques and smart little cafés. If you lived on the top floor, you let down a basket for letters and groceries. Now McDonald's, I think, is one of the first things you see when you get off the Eurostar. Oh, and the city was, I'm afraid, alive with the smell of urine. One took it for granted; it was very French. I thought at the time that it was so pungent because French people drank wine, which at the time the English didn't. But it was more that no one had seriously given thought to ways of disposing of the fluid. *Ou sont les pissoirs d'antan?* or *les boucheries chevalines d'antan?* (Can horse meat still be bought in Paris? For those big dogs, perhaps that Parisians have now.) Or *les concierges d'antan.* 'Concierge' now means something much more sophisticated than the crones who used to sit in cubicles at the base of the stairs keeping a keen eye out.

On holidays from Paris, I used often to go to Corsica taking the ferry over from Genoa. In fact the very first time I went to that lovely island was also the first package holiday ever. It was run by an entrepreneur called Vladamir Raitz. We were wonderfully housed in tents right among the pines that fringe the beach: two steps and we could be in the water beyond the tent flap. Corsica at this early time is wonderfully described by Dorothy Carrington in her book *Granite Isle.* We danced with Corsican fishermen at the nightclub called *Chez Tao,* paso-doble and tango. Outside, in the dark back alleys, dustbins were seldom collected and the church was still battered and closed. With my Corsican boyfriend Etienne I sometimes stayed in a high attic room that had a crucifix over the bed.

But then I made a wrong decision and came back to England (we didn't call it Britain then) to marry the English boyfriend. The marriage was disastrous and brief. During those few years, however, I had my two fine sons. We lived in a top-floor flat over an ironmonger's shop in Bloomsbury. In the flat below, a stout lady regularly got drunk and collapsed on the stairs; carrying one or other baby I would climb over her. I remember the lavatory freezing because of the cold (no central heating, of course). And I remember waking at five or six in the morning to feed a baby, shivering a little, looking out over dawn in a Bloomsbury street.

The marriage crashed. I became very depressed. And so I entered the jungle of psychoanalysis.

THE LONG VACATION

PART II

THE LONG VACATION

4. Psychoanalysis

(i)

Though the buses are crowded, most of the pilgrims to the shrine of the god Kataragama come packed into lorries piled on top with cooking gear and bedrolls. They camp, or are given shelter; cook their meals by the roadside and wash dusty clothes in the streams. From the car park stretch little streets of stalls, selling garlands, fruit for the offerings, and miniature spears representing the god. These can be driven through the face in fulfilment of a vow. The river is full of people splashing and washing, tipping water from bowls to the crown of the head. Round sacred bo trees, festooned with tiny flags, devotees are pouring on milk and water to nourish it. As it gets dark the elephants come out for the procession, decorated in elaborate coats and followed by drummers and dancers.

Dinnage, *New York Review of Books*

'My mother seems to hate me and I don't know why.' I sat nervously on the edge of the couch: to lie full length, with him sitting behind my head, seemed too bizarre. The analyst lived in a tiny flat up a lot of stairs.

I'd been offered a free place for psychoanalysis and agreed to wait until the children started school. But then it seemed I might have to move to Oxford after my mother's death, so I had started, at full payment, with someone who could fit in times around them. 'You'll soon feel so much better, you'll be earning more and finding the fees easy,' said the consultant. 'You'll like the man I'm sending you to: he's very intelligent and very *nice*.' (This puzzled me: were there psychoanalysts who were *not* nice?)

I didn't like him: I adored him.

THE LONG VACATION

(ii)

Later, when I forced myself uneasily into lying down, I could see a mantelpiece with a jar of pencils and oddments protruding (what could they be?) and part of a rather ordinary room. The couch was covered in a scratchy checked grey rug. I could see the tip of a polished black shoe reflected in the opposite wall. At once I set up an oddments-bowl on my bedroom mantelpiece at home.

I was thirty, a single mother of two boys, supporting us mainly by taking in lodgers: my own childhood at Rhodes House made me unwilling to leave them with carers. After they were asleep, I would be at my desk until midnight: hack work, sometimes translating books on speleology from French for £100 per book, no royalties. I learned a lot of French words for 'collapse', 'underground', 'inaccessible', 'echoing' and 'entombed'. I considered myself very old and with no particular future except that I would like to be less bad-tempered with the children. I wore sagging skirts and 'jumpers' (sweaters) from a second-hand shop, and maternity smocks cut down into blouses. I had one lipstick, an orange colour.

I've been asked if I'm *for* or *against* psychoanalysis. Is it that simple? In 1980 a balanced review I wrote of a rather anti-Freudian book by Frank Sulloway came out headed by the editor as 'The Genius of Freud'. This was precisely what it was not about. (Reviewers of course are never allowed to write their own headlines.) Odd. It isn't, surely, a question of faithfully supporting one team against another? I don't know the answer, so offer a new Jewish joke: 'For or against – what does it matter so long as he pays the analyst?'

And pay I did, out of a tiny income. It mattered so much: mattered because whenever there was a weekend or – worst of all – a summer vacation, I was back where I had been during the long university vacation at Rhodes House, counting out with the governess how many days till Mummy and Daddy came home. It always seemed to be forty-two. During the analyst's holidays I would determine to teach myself Italian cooking; make a skirt for summer; visit my father and his second wife, a dear elderly lady who had been a family friend. But the slowness of time, the waiting and then still waiting, was intolerable. Later on, the great love affair of my life consisted of waiting for the telephone to ring, for there are parliamentary vacations as well as university ones. 'You can only love someone who is absent,' said a later analyst, in Paris.

And yet I don't remember that all this was talked about much in that three-year spell or in any other therapy, for that matter. Perhaps it's not really amenable to discussion, too total, too obliterating, too metaphysical. Absence. It's when you cry and nobody comes. It's when there's nothing rather than something. True, absence can have an end, term can start again: but is the returning person the *same* one who went away? I think now that a child can be truly doubtful about this. And if the returned person is someone different, is the child who waited still herself? Is the world ever safely recognisable?

THE LONG VACATION

Once after an Easter weekend, the analyst rang me to make some change to appointments. To hear the voice over the phone was a shock: of course I knew, theoretically, that he was still alive, but four whole days had passed, and there was meant to be a block of empty time before he (and I) came to life again.

At the beginning of the treatment (was it treatment?) I think I slept a lot and dreamed a lot. When he told me I was bringing him a lot of dreams as a 'resistance', I was taken aback. Those resistances! It seemed they crept into everything I said or did. But one dream that I remember from the time was a nightmare of white broken faces staring at me while I called, 'Where's the doctor?' – and there he was in the corner, in a white coat.

Asleep or awake, I believed I'd found the answer to everything and would never be lost again. I read poetry, and I wrote it. Wherever I went, I felt he could see me. I still find it hard to bear that when I'm on the street no-one is seeing me and making me real.

What we talked about I hardly know. I only remember the wilderness times of weekend and vacation, and those last ten minutes of each session which meant, 'I'll have to leave and go out in the street.' Vaguely I wanted to get 'better', 'get cured.' This was a forbidden word which made him cross, but of course I wouldn't be getting cured of my depression, my terror, my isolation, because that would mean that I wouldn't see him any more. And of course he must be there forever. Mustn't he? Somehow.

Because of childcare timing I had turned down the offer of free treatment, but now the analyst gave me the news that he could only see me after daytime hours; he was embarking on a course. So the children, after all, had to be left here and there.

Mark was seven. On the way home one darkening evening he put his hand in mine. 'I'll keep your hand warm,' he said, 'and you keep mine warm.' Yesterday he came with me to another of those hospital scans I have now: it was a comfort.

It was in the third year, I think, that things in the analysis became odd. My analyst told me, in an accusatory tone, that I was having affairs that I was keeping secret from him. Affairs? I believed myself to be quite old, quite finished, totally unattractive. I couldn't believe what I was hearing, I couldn't believe it either when he said I had been rifling through his private life in some way. And yet I couldn't think that this intelligent professional man had actually gone mad. I was back in Garford Road, three years old, being told that Mr Galbraith had heard me crying all the way from Carfax. You are told what can't be true.

I don't know what I said; I think I twisted and turned, and soon after this the analyst suggested that I take time off to consider whether I wanted to continue these sessions. I agreed. Then there was a strange week of extraordinary trust, and shifting around towards the future. I had let go of him and then rediscovered him and made him real and all would be well. I wrote that I *did* indeed want to continue working with him.

He wrote back to say no, I had broken off the analysis and it could not be recommenced. That small, neat handwriting. A mild autumn day.

The night before the letter came, I had had a dream: a body had been chopped into pieces and scattered about.

The puzzle in the dream was: where is the actual person when it's in bits?

This is the misery memoir part, is it not? And it's not quite finished. I went, for a year or so, to see a kind middle-aged lady analyst who put me together a little. I did very much want to be together so that I could go back to reassure him – yes, believe it or not – 'It's all right. I've survived. Don't worry.' I made the appointment, I went in fear and trembling, face to face and he told me again and again that I'd come back to persecute him. I came out to a phone box and rang the kind lady analyst and she said, 'I believe you. I do believe you're telling the truth, and you're not mad.'

But after this it was a long time, about six years, before I was at all recovered. I got very thin (two stone is too much weight to lose). I saw the shocked look on people's faces when they only half-recognised me.

But things did, in the end, move on, here and there: to new learning, better work, some new friends, the purchase of a tumbledown cottage in Wales. And yet I am sorry to find that even in 1968 I wrote a very honest and humble letter to the psychoanalyst who brought my life to a stop – not answered of course. Why, I think now, did I never write in anger and bitterness?

It was not long after that letter that I was scanning through the psychology shelves in our beautiful Hammersmith Public Library and found a book that had startling, rather frightening phrases in it. Donald Winnicott: I imagined him strong and perhaps fiercely moustached. One phrase in particular stayed with me: 'Silent or secret communication with subjective objects, carrying a sense of real, must periodically take over to restore balance'. It made perfect sense: got through to me at once. That 'sense of real' – it was what I wanted so much. Sometime lost, then found again.

Soon I heard that this trenchant thinker would be lecturing at a meeting in Scotland, and left the boys with my neighbour to go there, nervously, with a friend. I found him to be old, fragile, and hugely comical. No one else at the conference seemed to be laughing at him, however: all was solemn. The friend who was with me found out that he was fairly famous but rather disapproved of. By the other psychoanalysts, that is.

When later I teased him about his jokiness at the meeting, he admitted rather demurely that when he was away from London he liked to 'let himself go' a little. In the train on the way back I dreamt, appropriately, that there were two Donald Winnicotts, one inside my mind and one outside. 'Thank you for letting me into your dreams,' he said courteously, when I told him.

I wrote to him at last, asking him for an appointment and explaining something about myself;

> At the moment I can't remember the things you have written, but I know they have sunk into my mind and fitted things that I partly knew, and completely altered myself. They have given me an idea of why I have not got better, so far, through having analysis several years ago; the idea that because I am quite intelligent and neurotic, no-one will look for any madness or unrealness in me as well. I may be wrong about this being the reason. My idea of what I want to learn from analysis is this: how to stop moving; how to

breathe; how to start moving. This may be much too difficult; I am already forty now.

I was aware that he was elderly and rather ill, had perhaps retired, and if so, asked if he could recommend some other analyst. But he agreed to see me once a week for an hour and a half.

'Why didn't you come to see me earlier?' he asked. 'Because I was frightened.' He believed that I had had some kind of break-up long ago, and that I needed to go back to it. This was just what I had been afraid of. Hadn't I put in my diary, in one way or another, that there was a thick harsh false-skin that must be ripped away and that the real skin underneath was horribly painful? I don't think any of this did quite happen – the ripping – and, in any case, it had been some time before I could come to formal sessions. There had been calls from the secretary – a heart attack in a New York hotel, a recovery, another illness, a postponement. 'If only you'd come earlier', he said again. Yes, if only if I'd had the courage.

I don't much remember, of course, what was said in our sessions, any more than I remember them with the former analyst. I know that he would sit on the rug in front of the gas fire and cover his gentlemanly dark suit with fluff. I remember short dozes – he was old – and sometimes we listened to music. In my diaries, as well as the agonies, there was a theme that came up from time to time. 'A benign alive space.' 'Something not too far and not too near.' Auden's line again, 'O calm spaces unafraid of weight.' The dozes and bits of music and wonderings were, I think, that benign space.

Oh, and I argued. I have done so much arguing.

At about this time, some initials appeared in my diary, accompanied by exclamation marks and a certain atmosphere of something joyous. Telephone calls? Disappointments. Or not. A certain casualness about adultery. And after so long alone... Winnicott, unlike most psychoanalysts, was not very interested in hearing about sex; he was the babyhood man. And yet he unlocked something for me, and my friend Initials, as I shall call him, was to be in and out of my life for a long time.

Some joy had crept in: it was not look-we-have-come-through time. Perhaps the-worst-is-over time?

* * * *

'I'm afraid I have bad news for you' Mrs Coles the secretary had said. It was an early call. 'Yes, last night.' 'Would you like me to send you back your letters? Dr Winnicott kept them all, you know.' Two years of letters were in a file. Sometimes the date or a comment was added in the margin in his handwriting.

I had written and written, letters flying between Hammersmith and Belgravia, London W6 and SW1: not much of a distance and yet a huge separating one that must be made sense of and joined up. Letters to establish that someone absent could be 'present' nearby, could be alive and continue to exist in some other place. 'I'm in Oxford railway station', I would write, 'I'm in Crawford's Cafeteria eating steak and kidney pie'. Time and space must join. One morning I might wake up in a terrible rage: 'What do I do with rage?' A Sunday morning, church bells down the road ringing and ringing, interrupting and interrupting: 'Things crash in and scatter me, when my whole life's work is to get knitted together'; and still the children's breakfast to get and the washing to hang out.

The typing so faded, and my eyes now so strained.

'I dreamt there was a great hole in my flowerbed and everything I'd planned had smashed.' Dreams proliferated. Some sort of advice bureau was being run by Groucho Marx, 'but he's funnier than you and can roll his eyes' (a Winnicottian scrawl in the margin seems to claim he can wiggle his ears). I wrote about pain, terrors: 'ALONE. Crying.' I might discover a poem, Robert Frost's 'wonder of unexpected supply'; 'but then it goes away: there's probably nobody there. Probably nothing real. This is my illness'. Then, the years away: 'If you had known I was in Canada you would have come and fetched me.' And tomorrow, on the train to Wales:

> You know how it is for me when I leave home: I have to leave home to go and find home. The trick of it is to find you have got home inside you all the time, even miles and miles away: more likely, though, it fails and there is nothing. In any case it has to be tried over and over again. You know about this. So tomorrow I'm going away for a whole fortnight and I wonder what it will be like, what will I find I have got with me? Oh I wish I could stay in one single spot and not move ever. But I'm made to go on and on, I've packed all kind of things, sellotape, drawing pins, sewing cotton in three colours, deodorant, Wellingtons, and now I'm trying to pack some Winnicott.

'Can anything be done for me?', I had added. It was done. Enough? Almost. I don't know.

So Winnicott died. I didn't cry, except for one second of the first notes of the *Moonlight Sonata* at the memorial service. The analysts who spoke there were rather cool about him, I thought. But the paediatrician who had been on the wards with Winnicott said: 'However ill a child was, when Donald sat by the bed for a while, the child seemed a little better.' My friend Initials was very good to me; he came round and read, 'Fear no more the heat of the sun...'.

Then, oh then, of course he was rather bad (another woman) and left Britain for an important job abroad. I went to hospital with cancer. Disgracefully, I visited him from time to time in New York and was perhaps a nuisance. He was away for a long time. When I was in hospital, my friends at the TLS were full of kindness – visits and cards and letters that I've never thrown away.

Years ago, I thought, 'If I ever wrote a memoir, I would start with the ward at the Royal Marsden, after the lights were out.' A sweet quietness, benign space. Fears quieted, murmurs hushed, a forgiving dusk. Like Winnicott's consulting-room.

(ii)

In this session we had roamed over the whole field between subjectivity and objectivity, and we ended up with a bit of a game. She was going on a railway journey to her holiday house and she said: 'Well, I think you had better come with me, perhaps half-way.' She was talking about the way in which it matters to her very much indeed that she is leaving me. This was only for a week, but there was a rehearsal here for the summer holiday. It was also saying that after a little while, when she had got away from me, it will not matter any longer. So, at a halfway station, I get out and come back in the hot train, and she derided my maternal identification aspects by adding: 'And it will be very tiring, and there will be a lot of children and babies, and they will climb all over you, and they will probably be sick all over you, and serve you right.'

D. W. Winnicott, *Playing and Reality*

In a book which came to life after its author had died, Winnicott refers to the 'Third part of the life of a human being, an intermediate area of experience to which inner reality and external fact both contribute.' From here, he says, image and myth and dream can grow, as they cannot in Freud's strict demarcation of true and false.

Is survival after physical death something 'to which inner reality and external life both contribute', or is it simply an illusion? When it is in spiritualist terms of comforts and heavenly choirs, certainly illusion. When the Society for Psychical Research, of which I have long been a member, was founded, post-Darwin, by a group of Cambridge dons, they hoped to find evidence for survival and perhaps a return to religion. A leading member, Frederick Myers, did arrive at a faith in post-mortem existence: he had lost a dear friend who had died young. It was part of his belief in what he called the Subliminal, something he proposed not long before Freud's Unconscious.

But most of his colleagues remained undecided. Much convincing material was amassed by the Society about precognitions, visions, telepathy, odd phenomena – I can never understand how people can simply dismiss these – but assurance about a true personal survival remained elusive.

So while Winnicott was alive I could 'tune into' him in his absence, talk to the image I had of him in imagination, but from the time of his death, this switching-on stopped: it was as if there was no current. Experimentally, I tried to write him a letter, but it failed, seemed to go nowhere. 'Please help me to imagine you. I seem to be against a sort of wall of mist that's solid.' But no, he had died, and I didn't believe in survival.

And yet...

There were, in this after-death time, appearances and disappearances in my imagination – not ghostly ones at all. In a garden in southern Spain, there was a monumental stone statue where birds perched that was, for some few minutes, Winnicott. Some time later there is in my diary the rather ridiculous entry: 'Remember Hyde Park Corner'. Remember? As with anything that feels somehow paranormal, clear remembering is just what's impossible. I think that at the Hyde Park Corner bus stop – not far from Winnicott's home – he for some moments? seconds? was *there*.

Then there was the voice. I shall describe later what I mean by 'hearing voices' and 'seeing visions' (not at all what psychiatrists mean). This was a clear voice, at the fruitful time between sleep and waking: 'I want you to bring me back.' It sounded very *ordinary*, neutral and unimpressive: I was not startled by a 'voice from the beyond', or clinically interested in a 'message from the unconscious'. It was not precisely real nor unreal, neither him nor me; so I assign it with a sigh of relief to Winnicott's all-important intermediate area.[15] (After my father's death I had no such messages. I simply became convinced, for the space of about six days, that after the funeral I would be marrying his doctor, whose name I actually didn't know. So it is possible to have a mini-insanity instead.)

And there was the third splendid re-finding. *Playing and Reality* came out some time after its author's death. I bought it and skimmed through the case-histories, always the most interesting part of psychology books. I was surreptitiously hoping to find myself described in there, described of course as the most interesting and lovable of

---

[15] 'No claim is made on its behalf except that it shall exist as resting place for the individual engaged in the perpetual human task of keeping inner and outer reality separate yet interrelated.'

THE LONG VACATION

patients. It's a totally engrossing book, but I saw nothing about my time with Winnicott.

And then I found it, some pages long: the re-creation of a session that we had. Our talk, he had written, drew on 'the vast area between objectivity and subjectivity'. Did it? I've no idea. I think we chatted about a dream, about a man I was falling in love with, about terror and losses, parting and disappearances, angels and eagles, family illness, a dog called Toby, truth and lies; about silence. We joked – why wouldn't we? – a chunk of our nice silliness appears at the head of this chapter. I did say 'reality is more important than comfort'; I remember that.

So I found in this posthumous book myself recreated, himself recreating. Words gone, words recovered. Words misremembered, even, (there is something about a cat) which makes them the more authentic and treasured. Could this be one of the most extraordinary things that ever happened to me?

5. *Exploring*

A blue jay lights on a twig outside my window. Momentarily sturdy, he stands astraddle, his dingy rump towards me, his head alertly frozen in silhouette, the predatory curve of his beak stamped on a sky almost white above the misting tawny marsh. See him? I do, and, snapping the chain of my thought, I have reached through glass and seized him and stamped him on this page. Now he is gone. And yet, there a few lines above, he still is, 'astraddle', his rump 'dingy', his head 'alertly frozen'. A curious trick, possibly useless, but mine.

John Updike, *The Music School*

THE LONG VACATION

(i)

I had, now, lost the analyst, lost the lover to New York, lost – in the Royal Marsden Hospital – my health. Another complete crash? These middle years were sometimes so sad that I wondered whether chemotherapy knocked out energy for a long time. I hopped from one oddball 'group' to another, tried a variety of antidepressants. This kind of thing was going into my diaries:

> Behind everything, the terror is going on: as though just behind a screen people are screaming silently and hurled off cliffs and cut by sharp swords into pieces.

Yet the single-parent household plus lodgers and children had been a friendly place for them. In those days neighbours knew each other and children romped through each others' gardens. I got a surprise note one day through the letterbox, from the blind Catholic lady next door. I have it still, crumpled and dirty. It ran something like this: 'I often see you come out and you look so sad. We are having a special day at the church. Father (who?) is very comforting and would welcome you.' I didn't go to see the Father (though I always loved seeing his Corpus Christi procession pass – the cross, the bearers, the children in white) but I have never let go of the letter. Miss Hunt shared a room with her friend in the Catholic household, and one morning the friend fell with a heart attack. Nobody sent for a doctor till late evening, after Miss Hunt had sat through the day in her darkness. Ambulances arrived. Because the two old ladies were a lesbian couple, relatives decided they must go into separate care homes. As now, I hadn't a car, getting to visit was horribly difficult; even more so, to bring the two together.

But in these later years, no longer much tethered by childcare and poverty, I began to make my way, at the least, to a respected place on the fringe of the literary world. As the no-hoper single parent of thirty, imagining myself published in distinguished literary journals would have been impossible. And I was dabbling in oil painting, starting a picture collection, dreaming *in colour*! How confusing it is that an *up* slope can balance *down* slopes! From the files of those years paper on paper falls out: scripts, bibliographies, translations, cuttings, offprints, prefaces, photocopies, titles, addresses, stories and poems.

And rejections. Much was unpublished. There was an unfinished book, that somehow connected with those half-heard words: 'I want you to bring me back'. It was to be called *Symbolic Energies* and to integrate Winnicott with some other ideas, fit jigsaw pieces into a design that I knew was out there somewhere. It was beyond me. Another semi-book, I should perhaps have persevered with: my attempted survey of pre-Freudian writings from around the turn of the 20th century gained me a friendly agent for a while and one publisher's rejection (I didn't know then about wondrous Harry Potter's thirteen rejections).

The short stories were odd ones. About endings: how a tiny thing finally snaps. About creating: how a creation comes to rule its maker. About destruction, how quick, easy and final it is. About people: so formidable, immense, like machines with confusing knobs to turn. But gradually, notes about real people began to appear – neighbours, friends, faces glimpsed in the street.

'Rather slight', a kindly publisher opined: nowadays who would bother even to send a note?

Once, for space and quiet, I rented a room for a fortnight in Earl's Court. It was very empty and cost, I think £3 per week. I could write absolutely nothing. The 'writing block'. Has it been studied enough by psychology? Is it just a fluency block, as my kitchen tap has, or something more deep-rooted? Why does it take so long to even partially dissolve it?

When I was back from Canada, some other ex-evacuee had evidently just written a not very kindly account of his story. My mother wanted me to contradict it by a more favourable account and handed me paper. I remember staring at its absolute blankness.

But the bits of writing strung me together, and the scribbles and the dreams that I faithfully recorded when I woke. I got into book reviewing, I think, by applying for a job at the *Times Literary Supplement*. Arthur Crook, the then editor, turned me down but gave me some unimportant books to keep me quiet. Unimportant tends to mean first novels, terribly difficult to review because nobody wants to be unkind to beginners. And psychology books, naturally, hard to find reviewers for them. All these humble offerings were at first anonymous, of course.

There was a history behind my getting published first of all as a reviewer. When we lived in the attic flat in Marchmont Street, I used to push the pram over to Gower

Street to deliver my then husband's copy to the *Spectator*'s office. And, later, didn't I once ask my father (an occasional reviewer for them) whether they might try me out? Oh, so timidly. 'Impossible, my dear. It's terribly badly paid. You wouldn't want to do that.'

I was probably, at the time, single-parenting in a typing pool or scrubbing kitchen floors. Funnily enough, the *Spectator* is one of the few journals I've never written for. Too right-wing for me.

I wonder whether in my reviewing I may have been trying to soften the rather stern criticism I always felt hovering at home into something more benign? I think I've always been fair and if I've found a book dreadful or difficult have avoided it. Salman Rushdie, for instance – no, not dreadful or difficult, indeed brilliant – but beyond my competence and understanding of the background.

I wish my university essays hadn't been thrown away along with my letters from Canada. Embarrassing they might have been, but I'd like to know where I'd got to by then. The rule conveyed to us in tutorials that we must not give an opinion without providing the quotation to back it continued. The wonderful, or funny, or even awful bits of the work under review seemed so much more interesting than anything I could say about them.

When John Gross took over the editorship of the *TLS* he gradually abolished the anonymity rule for contributors. (The idea had been, I think, that anonymous reviewers could safely be nasty about their colleagues.) What don't I owe John for picking me out of the slush pile of un-famous writers and pushing me forward – eventually to New York and dear editor and friend Barbara Epstein at the *New York Review of Books*! Actually the first serious piece I contributed under his editorship did happen to be anonymous. It was on the Freud/Jung letters, taking in the dreadful, the explosive divorce between the two giants, which has now been filmed:

> Your technique of treating your pupils like patients is a *blunder*. I am objective enough to see through your little trick. You go around sniffing out all the symptomatic actions in your vicinity, thus reducing everyone to the level of sons and daughters who blushingly admit the existence of their faults. Meanwhile you remain on top sitting pretty.

This was, of course, from Jung to Freud. Three months later, in 1912, came his letter of resignation.

Being a reviewer was not just a source of fun and anecdote; it was an education, almost equal to another degree, I believe. Of course books on physics should be reviewed by physicists, and a history of Manchuria by the appropriate specialist. But general books can surely be assessed by someone with a bit of knowledge and skill, a representative of the reading public who learns as well as writes. A review of mine was only once challenged – it was on a book about the mysterious Gurdjieff/Ouspensky group – extremely fascinating people. 'What makes you think you're equipped to write about this?', a member of a group asked me. Surely as equipped as the intelligent reader, and willing to write (and publicise) your group's book for a pittance, was what I thought.

THE LONG VACATION

Fiction I covered from Anita Brookner to Iris Murdoch (two ends of a spectrum) with a divergence to my hero John Updike. Having played about with unsuccessful short stories and poems was a help in understanding how far, far different were these real writers. Biographies are what I've liked best. (When I say 'liked', I don't mean that every step towards my desk wasn't a groan; I write so, so slowly. 'It's like putting your hand in a gorse bush', said Virginia Woolf.) I learned more abut Einstein and Darwin, for instance, than I'd gleaned before – as husbands in particular. About Dodgson the indefatigable paedophile. Mostly, though, I was sent biographies of women, though I can't see why women should only review their own sex, or men theirs. At the serious end, heartbroken Simone Weil; among the comics, Enid Blyton, creator of Little Noddy, and Marie Stopes the contraceptionist, prone to bringing out rubber goods for inspection at dinner, but an enormous emancipator of women nevertheless. Families: Gwen and Augustus John, orphaned artists, and in particular the James family. It is rare to have documentation linking grandfather, father, two famous sons, two 'inferior' ones, and a neglected sister. And William James was a member of our Society for Psychical Research, where I've belonged for the past thirty years. Henry, in fact, read a paper of his brother's to the Society in William's absence. Bizarre! The cut-glasss accent that William would have hated!

Some of the *NYRB* reviews were wonderfully illustrated by their caricaturist David Levine: Clementine Churchill cradles her husband's head as if it had just been guillotined; Danish writer Isak Dinesen (headline 'Gothic

Sybil') has hands you wouldn't want to be grabbed by on a dark night.

Once I actually wrote a *sermon* for the *The Times* itself. Towards the end of the *TLS* week, Patrick Carnegy, in charge of *The Times*'s 'Saturday Sermon', would appeal around the office for someone to fill this awkward corner. My piece on Van Gogh was editorially headlined 'The painter who brought light out of darkness' (*The Times*'s headlines were always wide). He had given up his ambitions to be a preacher in order to paint but; nobody bought. Before he killed himself he had written of his paintings that 'even in the cataclysm they retain their quietude'. They do.

I sometimes felt swamped by the Freudian books. Paul Roazen, historian of psychoanalysis, would take me out to an economical lunch in the hope of getting a good review from me. He mentioned the analyst Helene Deutsch. 'Oh yes – wasn't there a biography of her?,' I said, 'Yes, I wrote it, and you reviewed it.'

For a time I reviewed for the *New Statesman,* which everyone then read; Martin Amis was the young literary editor. At first I was sent dull and ordinary stuff, but it got a little racier. Lives of prostitutes. Pornography by Anaïs Nin. Victorian sexuality. A high point was when a newsagent's poster screamed 'ROSEMARY DINNAGE ON SEX AND VIOLENCE.' (it was actually a book on the suitability of children's television). I like to think that Amis and his crew had a bit of a giggle; I was very, very middle-aged. If only I had had the sense to get a copy of that poster.

The *TLS* itself had its eccentricities. Poems were chosen for publication idiosyncratically: John would seek opinions at random from anyone in the office. I sent one in myself, under a pseudonym: it came back by return post. *TLS* parties were... sometimes odd. John would wander round the office asking for suggestions of who to invite: 'Tom Conti!' fluted Victoria in her whimsy-flimsy way. On the day, the actor stood nervous and puzzled – why was he here? People sat on desks, spilling drink on copy from serious academics. Important gossip, I'm sure, was transacted. We were, those of us who just assisted editorially, a bunch of very intelligent people doing quite routine work – where a small error, nevertheless, could be disastrous.

My own deep shame was the *historismus* affair. The great art critic Ernst Gombrich had sent in copy (tattered and rough-typed as it always was then) using the word 'historism.' Historism? I asked around, consulted an enormous volume of the dictionary; people absently agreed it must be changed to 'historicism'. I should have telephoned Gombrich, of course. When the issue came out on Thursday, I was called in the editor's office. As someone once said about interviews with my father, it was like being up before the magistrates. 'Gombrich says he will never write for us again.' *Historismus!* Widely-known German art-historical term! Outrageously changed without permission! Possibly he never did write for the *TLS* again. All the same, I stubbornly continue to think: there is no such English word as 'historism'.

I enjoyed the Freudiana. Freud and women; the Berggasse apartment, the couch, Freud and the Jeffrey

Masson scandal; his letter to Jung's mistress, Spielrein; his crew of faithful supporters (some rather wonky); even Ralph Steadman's *Who's Afraid of Sigmund Freud?*, a bundle of loving, cruel caricatures, 'Analyze my drawings' wrote Steadman there. Didn't I just! The heading formed of knotted penises, bulging nipples, probing tongues, castrating teeth; the topsy-turvy classic Jewish jokes; Freud explaining libido under a potted palm to a lovely young lady, or at the Burgtheater, nearly obliterated by a matron's baroque hat. The Prater, the Schönbrunn Gardens, the very shape of the coffee cups at the Café Landtmann. Over all, Steadman's savage, inky-looking blotches and scratches. Aggressing the innocent paper.

Because of the person I was, of my attraction – sometime unwilling – towards the 'isness business', the inner-world stuff, I was even able to learn something about madness from reviewing. From 'outsider art': the fascination, from the 1950s onwards, with collections of works by painters who were either literally living in asylums or eccentrically withdrawn from ordinary social norms. Klee, Breton, Ernst, all of them were jubilant about the genuineness that was only to be found outside sane boundaries. Sadly, it wasn't there. Though Rimbaud had famously prescribed a 'long, prodigious and rational disordering of all the senses', wherever liveliness did show through these outsider pictures, it was due to talent. What showed much more strongly was the extreme restriction and loneliness of the 'mad' artists, hemmed in on the paper by tight lines.

Even more did this terrible isolation show in Daniel Paul Schreber's extraordinary *Memoirs of my Nervous Illness*. Published in 1910, it must be the most written-about document in all psychiatric literature, saved from obscurity by chance, admired half-jokingly by Freud and Jung ('he ought to have been made professor of psychiatry.')

Schreber had the ill fortune to be son of a renowned German authority on child-rearing, the author of some thirty books around the subject and founder of *Schrebergärten* playgrounds. Schreber père's system could well have influenced the generation growing up to be Nazis: control, obedience, suppression are to be obligatory. 'The idea should never cross the child's mind that his will might prevail'. A German friend of my own generation tells me that she and other children were still being threatened by the Schreber *Geradehalter*, a contraption of boards and straps, if they slouched at the dinner table. There was a published system for everything: the cold-water system, the gymnastic system, the lifelong diet system. There were two children in this family: one committed suicide and one went mad.

This one grew up to become a judge; he first broke down in middle-age. The *Memoirs* were written while he was in Sonnenstein public asylum. Has any other 'mad' person been able to set down his experiences with such clarity? The world population had been extinguished, he wrote: only corpses were visible. Rays and magic assaulted him, fragmented and annihilated his soul. Hallucinatory figures were secretly invading his body. He had no watch and as his shutters were closed at night, even the stars had exploded. The asylum director ran his kingdom with equipment – whips, straps, threats – much like those illustrated in the elder Schreber's child-care manuals.

The word that recurs in the *Memoirs* is 'forsaken'. The patient was forsaken by wife, family, friends, and in the end – what option? – by sanity. So too were the outsider artists intently cross-hatching triangles and squares on their scraps of paper. The forsakenness that drives people mad reminds me of Laing, trying to reach out to the insane so much later.

It will be a shame if Laing gets dismissed as a remnant of the hippyish '60s. Reading *The Divided Self* I had the relief, like so many readers, of disentangling some of the current misty ideas of 'real' and 'self' – an abyss of mystification that had frightened me was mapped out. Like Freud himself, Laing was drawing on nearly a century of fascination with selves and under-selves and inter-selves, with identity and its splitting, from Matthew Arnold's *The Buried Self* and Hopkins's use of 'selving' to the existentialism of his own time. I had glimpsed the outline of this abyss, safely and without jargon, during my short but fortunate time with Winnicott. (There was a debt here that Laing never quite acknowledged: 'Isn't it wonderful that Laing is spreading these ideas', Winnicott had said to me with a touch, I think, of wistfulness. Or sharpness?).

Laing gave us the idea that mystification and truth-deprivation can damage us even if we become only slightly mad. They are surely a kind of forsakenness? A long vacation?

Even without a horrific Scottish-puritan background such as Laing himself had, a child can carry a burden of mystification, what Laing calls 'the mass of confusion that is put over as the truth.' A generation of readers must have shouted 'Aha!' when they discovered Laing's word 'double-bind'. 'You *must*, though of course you *can't*' may be silently beamed across a family. Where does ordinary selving grow, between the two? 'I have had a lot of dishonest messages from people', I find in one of my letters to Winnicott.

It is sad that Laing paid the price – drink, divorces, trivial writings, pitiful public appearances, eventual expulsion from his profession – for that early Glasgow upbringing. He hacked a jungly path through to madness and the pockets of madness in sane people until he succumbed, under much pressure, to a kind of un-sanity himself. The 1960s and its crazes chewed him up and spat him out again. That he should ever be considered a druggy has-been is an outrage.

Reviewing these books was helpful to me when I was trying to befriend someone who had been diagnosed as schizophrenic. And perhaps reading them was relevant to my receiving a letter from an author thanking me for a review that had '*taught me so much*' (it was on Hermione Lee's wonderful biography of Virginia Woolf). I could understand Woolf's living on the edge of nothingness both from my own feelings, and from all this that I'd read. A letter like this makes every moment of the reviewer's work worthwhile.

(ii)

> There are some places here, thank God one finds them everywhere, where one feels more at home than anywhere else, where one gets a peculiar pristine feeling like that of homesickness, in which bitter melancholy plays some part; but yet its stimulation strengthens and cheers the mind, and gives us, we do not know how or why, new strength and ardour for our work.
>
> Van Gogh, *Letters*

There was actual travel exploration for me then, of course: everywhere I could afford, I went to. Travel writing can be less exciting, I know, than the thing itself. There was nothing boring, about paddling a dugout alone across a lake in Nepal, under the peak of the Fishtail Mountain. I'd been an expert canoeist on Lake Algonquin – but suppose in mid-Nepal I'd dropped the paddle? Would I ever have been found? ('Paddle your own canoe' is a maxim that I must have picked up in Canada.) One of the psychoanalysts said I travelled in search of my parents.

And visiting the ruins of Mycenae, again alone, in the time before Greece became a tourist destination. You had to take a train – very old and rickety – from Athens's unfrequented station and get it to stop at the right place, then climb a steep hill. The whole site was wonderfully empty. No tourist coaches. That Greek trip cost some serious sum like £100. 'But surely it was worth it', said Winnicott incredulously, 'to be up there alone?'

Ajaccio, later: glumly arriving in Corsica in the dark, and flinging open shutters on a dazzling harbour in the morning. Mykonos when there was only one hotel and no boutiques: at the top of a hill, a little boy picked an iris and offered it to his first tourist. That was true *filoxenia*.

Cooking fresh lobster on a beach in Maine. An old man, in Dominica, drying his coffee beans in the sun, roasts and grinds them and gives me a superlative drink. Swimming over the side of a rowing-boat in the Douro river, below the vineyards. Beethoven played in a painted wooden church in Norway. Sleeping on deck off the Turkish coast, woken by the call to prayer at five. Teenage wanderings in Italy: train supplement takes my last lire, meals bought by charming young men all the way to Victoria. Cycling down a Welsh hill towards a coast full of dolphins and thinking, 'People who don't do this are *mad*'. On a hill in Avignon and writing in my diary:

> Sitting on the white rock – the fortress behind me; in front cypress, olive, cherry, cactus, pine, thorn: tower, wall, road turning, rooves (browned) running round to fit curves. The straight river: circle of mountains very far away; it is like this: there is always the next thing, I must find it, I must go on to it, I must see it; and when it's there it is hard, bitter, lonely, beautiful; it fits me and is strange, totally, to me; so there is always the next thing, the lonely and beautiful, and the need, violent as this wind, to go on to it; this is the lie of the land, the contour of me, not to be changed; but here and there crops can be grown, things flower.

THE LONG VACATION

* * * *

The dreadful Atlantic crossing in 1940 and post-war primitive Channel crossings – bunks with a bowl underneath each one – haven't seemed to put me off travelling on water. So many of my journeys have been on boats. When the other day I got a great whiff of engine oil from an open garage, I was for a moment back on board somewhere looking for adventure. I've been up East Anglian creeks, around the Hebrides in search of Stevenson's David Balfour, as well as the Dodecanese and Ionians, sailed out of Venice, Split, Dubrovnik. Given my lifelong tendency to melancholia, there were surprisingly few collapses once I was away. There was one bad time, though. It was in Africa.

West Africa – Senegal and Gambia – was my only venture into the continent. Senegal had been colourful, cheerful: there was some kind of festival going on, with dancing in costumes that I coveted. From the circle little girls would step into the centre and try a few steps, getting the feel of dancing into their bones from the start. The cafés were suave, very French. But the Gambia, formerly a British colony, seemed different: slower, dimmer. An excursion had been laid on for us by the cruise company, down the river Gambia, wide and desolate. We were to visit an African village.

I don't know what, if anything, the villagers had been paid for letting themselves be exhibited, but they were desperate. Hands clutched my cardigan and tried to tear it off me. Something was being gabbled. They wanted – food, money, help, an explanation? There were movements in dark huts. The cattle – oh, this was worst – were all lying down, too thin to get up. Then we were shepherded back to our boat. The villagers, the Africans-on-show, stood in a silent unmoving block on the wooden quay as we floated away.

It was my birthday, I think, January. I cried and cried. A shipmate had somehow infiltrated my cabin; he didn't quite get it. Was it valuable for me, perhaps, to actually see African poverty, go beyond those photos of babies with swollen bellies? I believe the Gambia has luxury beach-side hotels now.

* * * *

India: (can't leave India out). I went three times, four if you count Sri Lanka as an only just separated appendage. One of these trips was to scout around for the *NYRB* – a ridiculously large task – the state of psychiatry in India. The patients I had the good fortune to sit in on were not all strikingly different from European ones. One man drank, one had become impotent; another felt 'weak', sleepless, tormented: there was depression without pills or much counselling. One woman was reminiscent of the patients seen by Freud and Breuer nearly a century earlier, who had physically expressed their misery in tics, paralyses, mutism. She twitches, the tall woman, and hears sounds

THE LONG VACATION

coming from all over her body, she says. It emerges that, under government persuasion, her husband has had a vasectomy. And she has no sons, only daughters.

A 'conversion hysteria' is not often seen in Western countries now. Everyone, I suppose, has heard – however vaguely – that mind can influence matter, that traumas linger on, that suppressed memory is hurtful. Whether we are any better for our half-knowledge I'm not sure. 'Man is in love with suffering', said the psychiatrist at the Aurobindo ashram in Pondicherry. Outside, birds were picking insects off the backs of pigs standing in sewage.

In Ahmedabad, further north, more industrialised and even more sophisticated, I was received with great generosity by a family who had known Gandhi (his first ashram was here) as well as some American psychoanalysts who helped set up a clinic, a family therapy centre, and day-care unit. East really met West here: psychoanalytic treatment could be carried out, and in what sounded like a more sensible and friendly way than the robotic 'I-am-blank-screen – project-your-fantasies-onto-me' style. Perhaps it has been influenced by the rather cosy local healers who I believe still flourish[16]. Accounts suggest that these have a good deal of success with their patients – not surprising considering research that's been done on the 'placebo-effect': an unexpected number of people, it seems, respond well to being given a pill containing no medicine at all.

An absolute contrast to part-Westernised Ahmedabad was Adyar. Just outside Madras, this great compound was

---

[16] Sudhir Kakr: *Shamans, Mystics and Doctors*

the headquarters of the Theosophical Society in its time of glory. The Society, casually started by roguish Russian exile Blavatsky, calmed by staunch English Besant, did much for India. Its doctrines were a muddle of misunderstood eastern mysticism, but its influence on the country cut through the colour bar of colonialism. Schools were founded, Indian nationalism applauded, and in 1917 Annie Besant was President of India's National Congress.

When I saw it years ago it was a great assembly of noble white buildings: all silent, all empty. Outside, a great banyan tree; below, the river where Krishnamurti and his brother were found and adopted by the Society as future gurus.

One day, standing on squashed vegetables in a market – Colombo? Madras? – I knew. 'No more Third World. This is the last time.' Squashed vegetables and a far paradise. And yet always the best bit was coming home. 'When I get to Spain, you'll come and fetch me home; then perhaps I'll go to Spain for a holiday', I had written to Winnicott. 'Fetch me home': from the Children's Home in Kent, from the hospital, from the times I ran away? And from across the wartime Atlantic, of course. Every journey was as joyful as opening a new book. And yet it was always an exercise, too, in being able to reach home again, in proving that *Here* and *There* are connected. That separation is a navigable trail – a lake, a portage, a tent, a campfire, a sleep.

And always there was the cottage on the Welsh border that was mine for twenty years. Opening the door at dawn, woken by sheep, and looking out across the valley below: smelling smoke and damp and sweetness, dew still on the grass. Neighbour's pig in the shed, apples in my orchard – my brother drove a load back to London that lasted all winter. Cock-crow from somewhere very far. A stirring and brightening. My piece of land.

Though the house was named from the hazel wood, the nut trees were too high for me to pick from and the cherries were pecked out by birds. But through the rough grass of my lower field, where Mr Roberts had hacked at cabbages, his sweet williams still came up. Beyond the hazels I could climb a very steep path to the top of the Deri mountain and see over towards Brecon with Blorenge and Sugarloaf rising on either side.

Before I had the money to lay a water pipe, the kitchen taps would splutter and dry up by July as the spring failed; then the Council would trundle up a bowser of water, to be used in careful bucketfuls. Neighbours were generous to me as an English invader, though not always to each other: at the bus stop one might have to stand between Mr Jones and Mrs Probert, not on speaking terms because he came from over the Hereford border.

Then through the day I might dig, paint doors, sweep up spiders, burn nettles, hang out washing. Take a cup of coffee out onto the bench by the ashes of the bonfire, listen to music and watch the swallows dive. Abergavenny no longer has shop window displays of rakes and seed and enormous Wellington boots; the weekly market has less home-made damson jam and more fake Victorian knick-knacks. No one walks three miles into town now to sell a tub of cream, a cream that is simply not to be tasted any more. There is talk even of moving the cattle market to Talgarth. There is a supermarket, a bookshop, cashpoints. A Chinese takeaway.

In the end I had to sell the cottage, and I shan't be able to see Cwmyoy's crooked church any more, or the holy spring at Partrishow. Though I could do with a holy spring now for the pains of old age.

THE LONG VACATION

(iii)

I think I'm justified in calling my long membership of the Society for Psychical Research a bit of an Exploration. Ghosts and ghouls, things that go bump in the night! I actually never saw or heard these and the sometimes creepy feeling of Rhodes House had nothing to do with it. I moved into the SPR at a time when I was researching my never-to-be-published book on late 19th century psychology. The group of Cambridge dons who set up the Society collected a mass of material on significant dreams, telepathic messages, poltergeists, premonitions. I wanted to know more. It was none of it irrelevant to the current movements in psychiatry and philosophy, even literature, that I was pursuing.

For the first ten years or so in the Society I read and read and learned a lot. I also studied the members with some fascination. What surprised me so much at first was that few of them, dedicated to their subject as they were, confessed to any paranormal experiences themselves. The psychic experiences tended to be for the lower orders: perhaps professional mediums, who are usually women. When I asked a parapsychology student who had a twin sister whether she ever had telepathic experiences with her twin, she said that she certainly did. 'But of course I never mention it in class or in lectures. It would be frowned on.'

We grow up believing in magic: fairies, Father Christmas, make a wish over your birthday cake. It's

THE LONG VACATION

lovely. It has to be grown out of, rather slowly and painfully, but of course we still hang on to it. 'We've had such a terrible winter, I think we'll have a lovely spring.' 'I've counted up to 100, there must be a bus coming now.' There's even: 'I love him/her so much, surely I'll be loved back.' Scientists won't touch this magical thinking with a bargepole, and psychiatrists want it extirpated from a rational life. I found that even members of the SPR still had some of this deep fear of regressing to childhood.

Having relinquished magic though, it's hard to accept that, for instance, a message can pass from one person to another without a sound, a radio wave, a computer. It's hard, I do see that; it's just that it's true. Lots and lots of carefully collected examples. Tests. Statistics. To give an account of 120 years of psychical research, consult the SPR library, not me. No satisfactory explanation as yet. Pretty rare, fortunately: I don't want anyone peering into my thoughts. I'm not in fact one of the members who impatiently wants to find a solution, to crack the code; we're probably better off in our ignorance. When experiments in 'remote viewing' were successful some years ago there was an immediate attempt to use it for espionage. But psychical research is a fascinating line of study, and enriches life. You have, of course, to walk a tightrope between gullibility and cynicism. As Elizabeth Barrett Browning wrote (she was an enthusiast, unlike her husband, author of *Mr Sludge the Medium*):

> It is easy to say 'humbug', and perhaps as easy to swallow the world and its follies whole by an 'omnivorous' credulity. But not to be either a stupid infidel or a credulous

hoaxee, is really hard, – where one's experience, and what one calls one's philosophy, lie on one side, and a heap of phenomena on the other.

She would have made a good intelligent member of the SPR, if she had not died some twenty years before its foundation.

I believe I said some while back that I would explain what I meant by seeing visions and hearing voices. That was rash of me. It was rash even to say above that a bit of psychical research enriches life. My own 'psychic' experiences have been so slight, so fleeting, so laughable to sceptics. And, as I've mentioned, so hard to remember: some rational part of the mind seems anxiously to fade magicky things out. I don't, in any case, see normal and paranormal as opposites with a brick wall between them, rather as a continuum with intuition somewhere around the middle; enrichment may just mean that, imperceptibly, one becomes more noticing of people and events and their interconnections. Coincidences, though usually random, sometimes seem patterned. The flashes of telepathy that happen so naturally when one is bringing up children – sometimes for the worse, as parental moods are hard to hide – might be discerned flickering still in adulthood.

Voices and visions: yes, I did, faintly, hear and see some. (Now, in old age, I can't even remember dreams – a terrible loss, worse than deafness and blurred vision.) Messages from 'voices' were wonderfully ridiculous. 'You're cooking for too many people.' 'Don't skip 'till the ground's dry.' 'Turned water into breathing-dust.' 'Talking with a threatening-machine.' 'You have been warmed/warned.'

There are sometimes these thought-provoking puns noticed by Freud: I've half-heard mother/bother, angry/hungry, treasure/pleasures. A black girl's face appears and says, 'I want you to be authentic and colourful.'

Hypnagogic sounds and sights surely come from the same region as symbols and poetic images: it's a question again of whether you label them normal or paranormal, where you place them on the continuum. Dreams drift into semi-dreams – and examples have clearly been noted where the dreamy message turns out to be verified by a factual event. The voices or visions feel so much from the *outside*, from Somewhere or Someone: so believed Joan of Arc, Socrates with his daemon, and innumerable prophets and mystics.

Mostly of course in ordinary sleep-dreams one is being robbed, cheated, delayed, threatened, despised – the usual stuff – hairdressers will make me look weird, people steal my shoes. And I'm endlessly, endlessly doing housework, scrubbing, sorting, sweeping, lifting, cleaning, carrying great piles from one place to another. As that's what I've spent most of my life doing it's natural, I suppose, to dream of it. The house-cleaning dreams have a rather pleasant sense of achievement, though, of sweeping out rubbish. In sleep-dreams I can even make jokes: 'My copy will be in late this week', I shout to an editor as a dream-wave engulfs me.

And the exam dreams! Nine o'clock tomorrow morning and revision not yet started. There was one of these where the invigilator told me very kindly that I'd passed anyway; this stopped the whole series. Freud, I believe, said that people who had exam dreams had usually done well in academic life.

Graham Greene dreamed as a child of the *Titanic* on the night it went down. Evelyn Waugh had a long dream of being very, very bored.

The SPR, anyway, was not really interested in dreams, visions, voices – images on the fringe of the paranormal. Members mostly didn't go out and explore séances as I did – and saw, I assure you, tables rising up to the ceiling in full daylight, voices speaking from under solid stone floors. Psychical researchers were too afraid of being accused of magical thinking and – let's face it – too snobbish. Professors don't attend suburban spiritualist séances. And when one member tried to push the Society towards contemporary publicity, there was a rustling as of Victorian skirts being primly drawn back.

Psychoanalysis and psi are not unconnected. Though his henchman Ernest Jones persuaded Freud not to admit it in print – there was already enough resistance to his shocking ideas (children interested in sex!) – he said late in life that if he had his time again he would investigate the paranormal. And he admits in some obscure source that when in sudden danger he heard a *voice* – not a thought – shouting at him to beware.

> I remember twice having been in danger of my life, and each time awareness of the danger occurred quite suddenly. I felt 'this was the end'... In these situations of danger I heard the words as if somebody was shouting them into my ear and at the same time I saw them as if they were printed on a piece of paper floating in the air.

The relation between patient and psychoanalyst is an unusual one – very close, yet frustrating – that can encourage telepathy. One half of the couple is probably deeply dependent on the other: he/she is a *patient*, someone ill enough or sad enough to travel to the analyst's home and pay money in the hope of being cured of pain. Cured by a *doctor* (whether medical or not) who has studied the mind, been to lectures and seminars and so must know much more than the poor dependent patient. This other half of the couple, the doctor, is taught to be totally reticent about his own life and feelings. A ridiculous rule (I understand it is somewhat relaxed now) which is supposed to bring forth important fantasies from the patient. Actually it may just make him/her feel rather bleak. Freud himself was quite affable with his patients, showing them his archaeological collection and occasionally taking one along on a family holiday in order to continue analytic conversation.

So there is a close but unusual bond within the analytic situation: the patient may well feel inquisitive about the doctor to whom she/he has confided so many secrets. And both are stirring up deep, half-forgotten feelings. It took me a long time to make a guess at why my first, disastrous analyst had ended the treatment in a way that so wrecked me. He had accused me of finding out his secrets, ransacking his files, spying on him. I now suppose that in the dreams that I obediently kept recounting, scraps of his own secrets were quite innocently appearing. Telepathy can work that way, I no longer doubt. Later on, something similar happened with a woman therapist. 'I was going to tell you something important today' she said to me, 'but I see from your dream that you already know it. I'm getting married next week.' No fuss, you see. No accusation of spying. I didn't even know that I knew it.

Exasperated opponents of psychical research will argue: if people can 'know' things, why don't they win all the lotteries and get very rich? Because it's not like that. Psychic intuitions are unreliable, fleeting, connected with deep emotions. Coincidences muddle in with them. Fairy godmothers are lovely, but belong in fairy stories. There are, I admit, things on the fringes of the paranormal that I don't attempt to either believe or disbelieve. We don't know enough – less than the Victorians did – about things like hysteria and dissociation and hypnosis, even about imagination, what it is and can construct. There's a lot more to learn; but I think it's more comfortable to probe no further.

One thing I do have no doubt about: precognition. This is a tough one, because it rubbishes our conception of time. Yesterday: Today: Tomorrow. Tamper with that at your peril. And yet I have so often found that something unmistakeable (but perhaps trivial) from a night's dream appears during the following day that now, when I wake with a surprisingly happy dream I predict it will be a good day. And vice versa, of course.

* * * *

Buddhists accept the paranormal (sky flying, giant leaps, danger-messages from far village, visions of

Padmasambhava) but say that these are trivialities, mere distractions from the pure emptiness of meditation. (At least, so I have been told; perhaps not strictly true.)

When one of my mid-life explorations led me towards Buddhism, I was following a trend; everyone around the late 1970s, it seemed, was drifting that way. In California it had always been Zen; in Britain, where Tibetan exiles had fled via India, Vajryana was taught – more colourful, comical than the impassive Japanese version. Following fashion, yes; but isn't it odd that when in Oxford I'd been taken to the Indian Institute, aged nine, I went home chanting to myself the mantra '*aum mani padme hum*'? I distinctly remember it, crossing Holywell, Blackwell's being over the road where the giant library now stands. A serious Buddhist would say I'd been Buddhist in a former life. And I remember a conversation with Lord Lothian, the semi-uncle I was fond of as a child, about *whether it was possible to have no thoughts*. It was impossible, he said, to have nothing going on in the mind. I wasn't sure. But I was interested in the idea of that... void? Did I know the word?

And *meditation*, so constantly mentioned in those 1970s days. When I stayed with a nominally Buddhist family in Sri Lanka they couldn't grasp what I meant by it, though they were English-speaking. 'I don't think we'd have time for that', they said.

There was no particular crossover for me between an interest in psychical research and in Buddhism. And in fact in trying to describe the latter I feel as Flaubert did when he wrote: 'On Saturday I begin *Bouvard et Pécuchet*. I tremble before it, as on the eve of embarking on a journey round the world.' I can't really do it. I have no ineffable stories to tell. Oh, no. And I can't say that I'm still '*a* Buddhist' as one might say *a* Hindu or Christian. Or even that I sit down for twenty minutes a day in the lotus position (too arthritic now; what do old ladies in Buddhist countries do? Prepare soup for monks, I suppose.).

In my great stack of diary notebooks, mostly clogged with moans and dream-reports, I sometimes – rarely – note a phrase that stops me. 'The original, the blank, the pure and clear, free from cluttered newness'. 'Steadiness of the real world, as one is driven from the habitual world' (that one is Virginia Woolf). The habitual world – I think it's what Buddhism calls *samsara*. Rubbish, junk, noise, prettiness, chatter, flutter, buzz, flicker, scattering, boom, twitter, twizzle, strangle, groaningness. As I write, it's four days to Christmas, the great samsara season, I include something from my diary of forty years ago:

> Christmas shopping. The glitter, the noise, the crowds, the buffeting. Four o'clock in the High Street, getting dark. Birds fly overhead. Looking up: their height, strangeness, in a different element above all the noise, as though we were underwater and they above in the air. Their power, movement, sense of direction pulled by some force we can't feel. Our forces down in the crowd; theirs simple, different, above in the colder air.

I don't think I'd investigated Buddhism there but that was already the way I was looking, away from the darkening High Street. And I'd copied out (Auden?): 'O calm spaces unafraid of weight'. Some shrink or other, later, didn't understand the quote, as she hadn't when I said I'd dreamt

I was a path. 'Where were you going?' she asked. 'I wasn't *going*', I almost shouted. 'I *was* a path. It was a dream.'

If one must be psychoanalytic, this picture of stillness and clearness could have been created out of having a mother who alternately invaded and withdrew.

A retreat in Devon. It was *cold*. Freezing. Each member had a separate room; we met for the evening meal – brown sliced bread and butter at 5pm. No talking allowed. The trick of staying warm was to spread clothes under the top bed sheet to keep them out of the damp overnight. In the afternoons, Woodland Walks were allowed; I would hurry downhill to the village shop for a Mars bar. Why I thought it was a week well spent, I can't imagine. But damp, cold, living on Mars bars, it *was* well spent.

I'm shooting all around the target, I know, and can't get the centre into words. I'll try John Snelling, an English Buddhist I talked to some years ago for a book of interviews on death. Fifteen years earlier, at the age of thirty-one, he'd been diagnosed with leukaemia. He was appalled and disgusted and terrified:

> But then I began to really feel this thing in my body, and as it progressed I became more and more sleepy and more and more tired... And then the whole saga of that particular night was interesting, because although I went to bed with, as I say, these tremendous mingled feelings of anger and incredulity and fear – many things – I went through a kind of purgation in the night, through fear, in a way. I don't know what it was, but when I woke up in the morning I'd come to terms with it.

He quoted Dr Johnson: 'depend upon it, Sir, the thought that he is to be hanged concentrates the mind wonderfully.' I think probably it was the Buddhist practice John had already done, so hard and wearisome, that had concentrated him wonderfully. (How much I learned from interviewing people! Never mind that the books didn't sell well.)

And here am I, 84 and with death staring me in the face (oh, how horrible that phrase. Look away!). And I don't know whether or what I *am* concentrated on. Perhaps Buddhism was for turning the frightening nothingness into benign void?

'Our awareness is like a small baby', said Sogyal Rinpoche at a long-ago Buddhist meeting, 'thrown into the battlefield of samsara. We must cherish it.'

There's a problem too in Buddhism with the word 'ego'. An article I wrote on Tibetan Buddhism was editorially titled 'Let the Ego Go'. It's what the Buddhist writings keep telling you; but have I, we, got an ego to nobly discard? I have a wobbliness, a sharp eye, a terribly bad temper: is that ego? All those 1970s encounter groups entreated us to 'find out who you are'. We are not very sure. Psychologist Erik Erikson, fair-headed son of a vanished Norwegian father and an orientally dark Jewish mother, published books on *identity* for decades. Asian babies perhaps, so cuddled and unbothered by a training in self-sufficiency, have no trouble with the ego/*Ich*/self problem. For Freud the ego was to be striven for, was the charioteer of unruly horses. Certainly nothing to be got rid of. Though I can't find anything among my few books on Buddhism, there must be analyses of the Sanskrit origin of

THE LONG VACATION

these mysteriously powerful words – ego, meditation – and how they came to be translated in the West.

Back to samsara. The approach towards a Buddhism that I can't quite get into words was at the least an attempt to shift away from that wretched samsara. I have the most oppressively cluttered, unstoppably chattering mind in the world. It shies away from any gap in the noise. It keeps me awake for hours at night explaining things I already know, to people who don't exist. The doctor won't prescribe sleeping pills any more. 'An over-active mind' was diagnosed in my childhood. I know what Winnicott would diagnose: 'a fear of falling into nothingness'. Oh, why won't you come back and help me? Step into the nothingness with me?

It's not that samsara-ism itself is evil. I've an idea that one translation of it is 'everydayness'. It could be stirring porridge; humming; looking through seed catalogues. We need quite a lot of it. The problem is when it becomes an addiction. I don't drink or smoke, don't watch television, and modern radios don't work for me. (*Digital*?) It's printed stuff, I think, that samsara-izes me, that and the all-night discussions with non-existent people. Those Sunday papers, for instance: the colour supplements. I've just been trawling through a full page of *party handbags* (there are such things). One is large and gold. There's a tiny one on a chain. One is a pair of big thick lips. *I don't want any of them.* But these horrid things force me into spending a good ten minutes scanning each one, comparing, choosing, dribbling away precious moments of a life.

'Some spiritual treasure', is what John Snelling ended by saying; 'a pearl of great price, a hidden jewel'. Probably in all religions, he thought. Perhaps it means turning the frightening nothingness into clear space.

That's all I can find to say about Buddhism. Except that meditation – more usually called 'sitting' – is awful. It's... awful. Sitting. Sitting. Sitting.

6. *Ending Up*

THE LONG VACATION

(i)

I had often been back to Oxford, of course, for a struggle up Headington Hill, a walk through Christ Church meadows, a visit to Blenheim. But not to Rhodes House. It was time to do that.

How many times have I made the journey between London and Oxford and vice versa? Five hundred times? A thousand times? Being taken for the first time to the ballet, Markova and Dolin in 1935. Travelling down to take my son out from Wadham. *Up* to a Selfridges' sale. *Down* to lunch at the Trout Inn. The up train, and the down train! Railway lines don't change much. Trees bushier, new factories. Slough, where Betjeman aimed his unfortunate line, 'Come friendly bombs and fall on Slough'. Reading: glimpse of river. Didcot has sprawled, Radley and Appleford Halt perhaps gone. Dreaming spires harder to see.

I had been nervous of revisiting Rhodes House, knowing that inside the building much had been changed. I wanted the pictures in my mind to remain just as they were; had a list to check starting 'nursery, cellar, Lothian's suite, bike shed, rainwater tubs and grindstone, larders, cherry tree, sandpit, row of Spy cartoons, ironing-room, grand piano, log fire, cold radiators, airing cupboards'. Thick dark velvet curtains, for hiding behind. The secretaries' window, for jumping out of. And I would have liked deaf Emma (killed in the blackout) to be still there, and Amy, and Lily Jarrett and many scullery maids without names.

'You'll find Don the friendliest person you could meet', said Bob, the Rhodes House porter and driver who met me at the station, 'and I've worked for four Wardens. Four! I think you'll find the house the same in a way, though it's different.'

He was right on both counts. Don Markwell – about the age of my sons – is Australian as my father was (though my father, I think, worked harder at eliminating the accent. It was better, in those days, to be an English gentleman than a colonial).

Don had been a Rhodes Scholar, then a Fellow of Merton, then headed two Australian universities before returning to be Warden in 2009. He lives at the moment on his own, though his grown children come over from Australia, so the greatest change within the house is that it is quiet and... rather grave. Bob and his wife Dawn live in the attached Porter's Lodge. In, say, 1937 there would have been around fifteen people living in the Warden's Lodging, as well as daily secretaries and gardener.

I said earlier that Rhodes House, for all its splendour, was not ideal for growing children. Yet when I think of the liveliness, the comings and goings both before and during the war and all masterminded by my mother, it seems sad that the moment my father retired in 1952, the incoming couple declared the place *totally* unsuitable for their children. Huge changes were made.

So my first impression was quietness. The sculleries, pantry and huge kitchen were closed off. 'But the dinner parties, the receptions?' I asked, remembering waves of boring grown-up chatter that sometimes floated up to the nursery. 'Caterers are used', said Don, and no doubt there are ladies who clean.

Through the important door that in all grand houses separated the lower orders from the gentry, the hallway was reassuringly the same. Beautiful oak floors here as throughout the house, mahogany chest, portrait of Rhodes (a different one), carved Zimbabwe bird at the foot of the banister rail. But the sitting-room had been moved to the dining room and the huge sitting-room itself changed to Warden's study. Not good: no grand piano, no log fire? No place for Christmas tree? But Don was a welcoming host, and I a polite visitor.

I did decline to go upstairs; I understand that my parents' blue-and-white chintz bedroom has been turned into a dining-room and kitchen. I was sometimes allowed to go down there with them when Lily brought in morning tea. So no viewing of kitchen. But we explored the cellars that were once dark and spooky. The storeroom that held food against an approaching war now stores files. The one where, on only two occasions, we went to when there was an air-raid warning, holds – can I remember? – boxes and so on. There still seem to be some dark underground book stacks even though no-one to play hide-and-seek round them. The room that held the dressing-up box – tabards and crinolines and milkmaids' aprons from my parents' amateur dramatics days – stores more boxes? Files?

The real change is in the further part of this underground kingdom; beneath the Rotunda: pleasant modern studies and sitting rooms for Scholars. And above – lo and behold, something that would amaze my father! – Rhodes House lets out lecture rooms to wedding parties now, and in the Jameson Room (Leander Starr Jameson, leader of disastrous South African raid in 1895) where my father's portrait is, colourful guests in those weddingy clothes circulate with champagne. The Milner Hall (wartime dances to Victor Sylvester's Ballroom Orchestra on gramophone, happy schoolgirls, partners in Free French and Polish uniforms) has long tables laid out for what looks like a feast such as was never seen in 1943.

And above, I believe, is a library of very important books on colonial matters. I've never been in it.

Don Markwell throughout our tour has been very patient with my cries of 'That's where my rabbit died!' and 'Where's the grandfather clock?' But beneath his jovial Aussie ways, he is very, very serious about the Rhodes cause. He doesn't deny that Rhodes was a racist and an imperialist; even more than most in his time, he wanted a white, English Africa to add to our glorious Empire. He came, he saw, he grabbed. But Dr Markwell stresses, in particular, Rhodes's vision of future peace. There was a sense already at the time of his Will, says Markwell, of approaching hostilities. After talks with the Kaiser, Rhodes left the bequest for four German Scholarships per year in 1901.

Educational relations make the strongest tie, he insists. 'His vision, was that by bringing together clever young people who would have influence, bringing them to the collegiate environment of Oxford, they could promote good relations between the three Great Powers'. And this wish goes back a long way, he says, even to Rhodes' first Will of 1877 – 'which could otherwise be seen as youthful and naïve' – where he talks of making wars impossible. 'And one of the things that interests me', the Warden continues, 'is that in the first half of the twentieth century, which of course included the time when your father was Warden, the issue of international peace became more and more relevant. Even as a child in Rhodes House you may have become aware of some kind of increasing danger as the 1930s continued.'

Don talked also of 'life-changing opportunities', 'high calibre students', 'impact on the wider world', '83 young people a year', and he gave me a glossy colour booklet on the Mandela-Rhodes Foundation which I read on the train back. Mandela and Rhodes together! In the photos, the benign old man with his halo of white hair smiles among groups of young people of many colours. Graduates of African universities, they will win a period of further study, some of them in Oxford. What's not to like? And Don looks even further forward. Nigerian, Ghanaian

Scholars? Kenyan? Even Ugandan ('they have elections there now'). I know nothing of university politics but it seems to me, who grew up under the stern gaze of Rhodes at the foot of the staircase without any interest in him, it seems to me pretty good.

There have been, clearly, endless ups and downs, agreements and compromises, tangles and disappointments, skills and blunders, in the 110 years of administering Rhodes's Will. There are black Scholars now, of course, and women Scholars: Oxonians might be surprised to know that until 1947 there were neither.

Goodbye, then, and out across the Rotunda, with its echoes and marble floor and Latin inscriptions, to the Portico, topped by bronze Zimbabwe bird, noble, surveying misty Oxford. The black plaque on the wall announcing Mandela-Rhodes Foundation looks rather small and dark in comparison. No-one who walks down South Parks Road can miss the Portico and its massive pillars. It's unmissable. It's magnificent. It's inappropriate.

This is how we were, it blatantly says. When there was Empire. When my mother could talk of her 'nigger brown' dress, my father of 'working like a black' in his study, when Cecil Rhodes declared that 'I like land better than niggers'. There are no Empires now, only zones of influence and cold wars and realpolitik. Cecil John turns in his grave.

So keep turning.

(ii)

> It has taken me three years to understand this – to come to see this. We resist, we are terribly frightened. The little boat enters the dark fearful gulf and our only cry is to escape – 'put me on land again'. But it's useless. Nobody listens. The shadowy figure rows on. One ought to sit still and uncover one's eyes.
>
> *The Letters and Journals of Katherine Mansfield*

A final chapter should be full of wisdom, should it not? – of lessons learned, of advice to impart. Of being clear about the shape and value of a lifetime. Of a declaration that writing about oneself, contravening the childhood rule against 'I, I, I' and any claim to be the only pebble on the beach, is *not* vain, selfish, unjustified. It is even something like an atheist's version of the prayer for 'time for amendment of life' before death.

Advice to people younger is actually very scanty. Memory, one discovers while writing, is extraordinarily unreliable, quite eccentric even. Who was XYZ who keeps appearing in the diaries, or ABC? Did I really go to Ireland: when and why? What was it that in 1970 I declared to be 'unforgettable'? And in 1980-something what was it that was so upsetting? What did he/she really say to me that other specially fateful time?

THE LONG VACATION

And free will, decision-making. There seems to be so little of it (though a friend of my generation doesn't agree: Perhaps men do have more free choice). How could I have known, at twelve years old, that an adventure across the Atlantic would make me very sad? Later, why didn't I demand back the essays I lent before exams, and get a better degree? (I think I have the answer to that: I didn't want to excel.) What if I hadn't been to that party, that meeting? How could I have known that a psychoanalyst would go mad? An answer does seem to emerge as I write: it was because I never had any confidence. That's a bad basis for firm, crafty decision-making. Choices, I think, may anyway be made at some deep level that we can't access.

I could tell the young also that age is a time of being *frightfully angry*. For a whole lot of the time. Things dropped from the shaky hand are hard to pick up. People simply won't speak up clearly. Stairs get steeper, pavements more slippery. The only answer is to cultivate a *je-m'en-foutisme*: some eccentricity, however timid.

And yet...

A friend of mine said he wasn't quite sure what the word 'spiritual' meant. I expressed shock; but discovered that I didn't, after all, quite know myself. Then I found, looking through something I'd written, that I *did* know: the spiritual, I'd written, 'is a time when the structure of things can be seen, when trivia fall away, when purposes are lessened and feelings freed'. It's strange to find, in something you've written yourself, that you knew an answer all along without realising. Does this often happen? Do we all know more than we realise?

The sentence I'd written was in a review of *Kaddish* by Leon Wieseltier, an account of a rather reluctant year of ritual Jewish mourning for the death of his father. He wrote to me thanking me for my kind review, and marvelling that a woman, a non-Jewish woman, should have written it.

Most of us don't, if post-Christian atheists, have mourning practices or pre-death exercises we can carry out. And yet there is a sort of hunger for something spiritual in age: we're about to be crushed out ruthlessly, after all, dropped off as carelessly as dead leaves leaving space for spring. But: 'You must come to our church', said an Ealing neighbour. 'You'd love it. It's not a bit religious, honestly.' The present-day C. of E.? I don't think her church would ready me for extinction.

But to survive death in a sort of floaty way, as a few - very few - members of the Society for Psychical Research may still believe... I don't think, as described for instance in *The Tibetan Book of the Dead*, it would necessarily be desirable. After a funeral, though, there does seem to be – I hardly know how to write it – a sort of voice from somewhere. I've mentioned that earlier. Or a piece of music, sometimes.

James Horrigan, a staunch Catholic who was dying of cancer when I interviewed him for a book on death, had no doubts or fears but puzzled himself about the hereafter. 'I often sit and visualize what heaven's like. And I don't know! That's what. Do you know, I haven't the faintest idea!'

* * * *

There was at least a tradition of good deathbeds once. My hero Samuel Johnson feared death – he said that only those who were sure they had never done wrong did not – but he met it, says Boswell, with fortitude. That he, the most generous and good-hearted of men should have any fear of the afterlife, is absurd. The worst he did was to take ladies of the town to alehouses and chat to them. As he prayed and read his Bible, his friends gathered; he made Sir Joshua Reynolds promise not to draw or paint on a Sunday. He would take no opiates because he wanted, he said, to meet his Maker with his mind unclouded.

Joseph Addison, so much more tedious a person and writer, invited his friends round to 'witness how a Christian could die'. How the event proceeded we don't know. Johnson would never have been so self-important. His friends attended because they loved him.

In the *Guardian* recently there was a rather nice, short feature about a *good* death: I think someone rather important had died earlier than he should and had done very well in making for himself a quiet departure. I liked this: rather fancied the idea of having one of them myself. I toyed with words like 'serene' and 'plucky'.

In actual fact serenity, as I've said, is extraordinarily hard to achieve in old age. In a recent hospital stay, I was actually ticked off by a teenage, red-haired, Irish nurse because of my shouting one or two four-letter words when extremely painful things were being done to me. 'Don't you say those words in front of me!' Old age is all exasperation – and yet I did like that idea of a good death. Over one of my frequent sleepless nights I toyed with the notion of a very nice post-mortem message left to my grandchildren and presents that could be distributed among friends. I fell asleep peacefully after this – but then woke with an extremely horrible nightmare. So perhaps it is best not to dwell on rosy things too much; somehow some kind of balance is going to have to be arranged.

I was in hospital because of an operation on a painful arm, an operation that was meant to take an hour but kept me in for five days and has left me unable to type and scarcely to write. 'I'm not proud of myself', said the surgeon, the nearest he could get to an apology. So why this persistence, when it hurts just to pick up a pen? Is it to demand: '*Admire me*'? To round off a story?

Before the operation went wrong the doctors believed the arm had 'compartment syndrome'. So I was thinking quite a lot about compartments. Compartments in the National Health Service, one solid box never communicating with another. Compartments in the mind, one labelled Death and the other No Death. Have I succeeded in decompartmentalising the mind? Not really. Freud, I believe, said that biography and autobiography were impossible – real truths could never be discovered – and he was probably right. At best a shape, a storyline, a set of compartments imposes itself on the amorphous mass that is a lived life.

So much left out: can I stuff any of it in? Books read, I'd need another 100 pages for that: the exciting emergence, in the 1950s, for instance, of volume after volume of Boswell's diaries, discovered in an attic. Dance: dreams of floating down a staircase *en pointe*; first glimpse of flamenco. Politics, of course. And people, people, people; but they mustn't be betrayed by being put on a page.

And there's the melancholia compartment. I don't want it to exist, but as I wrote I constantly encountered it. The gap between the little appointment diaries filled with lunch dates and cinema times and the stack of big notebook diaries full of dark and fear and unrealness and separation. For anyone feeling guilty about having pages like these – and depression is now so briskly medicalised that there's always some shame about not being able to manage the happiness trick – I can only say that the gap *can* be handled. Well, some of the time. There is a loneliness, though, in having to be what Winnicott calls a 'caretaker self'. Dickens wrote of himself that there is an 'inner creature who is crying somewhere, by himself. At this moment I can't dry his eyes. He is being neglected by some ogress of a nurse. I can't rescue him.' I often dream –

do others? – of looking after a lost child, or straying kittens.

My hand hurts, and won't go any further. I'll leave, taking with me a small spiritual package, not a compartment. I would put in *Kaddish* and Keats's belief in 'the holiness of the heart's affections.' The Turner watercolour of three fishes, rather Buddhist-looking fishes – I think it's in the Tate. My family and my cats would of course be there and then I would put in a passage from an Iris Murdoch novel. It's a scene in a Quaker Meeting House, when suddenly an elderly man (he may have just received rather bad news from his doctor) stands up and to his own surprise speaks to the little congregation about a better way to live. To live quietly and patiently and with as much love as can be managed. Iris Murdoch, naturally dismissing Christianity as a collection of myths, was always looking for a sort of religion, a sort of holy focus, and she recreates the atmosphere of a Meeting House so well, as I knew it in Princeton in 1943. Somewhere in my package there would be a little Buddhism and a little Quakerism. 'To unite and pacify before the end'.

Perhaps I could borrow for myself from Murdoch the title of one of the books: *A Fairly Honourable Defeat*? If I had the timidest hopes of having got anything into words, it would be about connecting the 'inner' world and the ordinary one, for blurring the line between them.

In Andrew Solomon's *The Noonday Demon* he describes a collapse into depression when he became so ill he had to be fed by his father. Solomon was just able to say to him that he'd like to live long enough to feed his father in his old age if it was needed. The wish, he says, was perhaps 'the ropy fibre that runs through the centre of me, that holds fast even when the self has been stripped away from it.'

Yes, a ropy fibre, even stronger than those tough compartment walls, stronger than we are able to know. And perhaps it grew or was fed into us before we *could* know: some goodness more powerful than a limb swollen with poison. A fibre that once connected me, inside, to my sons, who are now so good to me.

* * * *

Very early morning. Deep summer smells. Leaning out of my bedroom window: the *ailanthus* tree, the copper beech next door in Wadham. Somewhere close on our side a woodpecker drills: farther down the road, a cuckoo faintly starting. It's going to be a fine day.

THE LONG VACATION

Fragments

The Leopard, at the end. The Prince leaves the waltzing, the glare, the music. Goes out into the night. Glimpsed in a dark hovel: woman and baby.

Somebody left the door open. In the gutter Maudie was dead, her kittens still in her.

Marché Ste Cathérine. Water bubbles up into gutters, pigeons splash.

Bakeries, Mr Nash, white with flour, comes up with loaves. In Plantation Road, they take loaves out on flat spades.

Nelly Quinn. She scrubbed the bath clean in three minutes. Had to leave Jersey quickly because she had a Jewish grandmother. Hated priests but wouldn't be without a drop of holy water in the house.

'In its hurt the soul isolates itself.'

Small white dog looks at me. Total innocence.

In the tight ugly pink roses, greenfly. Sticky.

A dream: I was walking on water, everybody watching in amazement. Abashed, I called out 'Only joking!' and sank.

Rooftops in Perugia, eight in the evening and pure fading light, old worn stone. Swallows swoop: little high screams. The signora calls us for supper.

I went here and there and didn't find you. The ways, the particularities of your being not-there. Each person's unique not-thereness.

Simon: 'Would an elephant suffocate in the Underground?'

A dream; I made a little man out of bread and it came alive, moved one arm, then both. I was very proud. I thought it might tell me what to do, but it couldn't.

The monastery in Greece at Easter: monk dancing with the shepherd at night.

The door slams and I wake up with beating heart. Think of the sheep's hearts I've sliced up for cats; strong twisted tubes. Broken heart. Heart failure.

November, small gas fires popping in darkening bedsitters. Crumpets.

The taxi-driver was a single mother. Best way to support the kids. 'I didn't love him, you see.' 'Yes.'

Joe in hospital: his appendix is out. 'That's a brave boy.' He doesn't speak, only nods or shakes his head.

THE LONG VACATION

Little boat speeding us out to Tresco. Sun and spray. I didn't know my loss till then.

Title for a painting: *Apple and Pear Living Quietly.*

Enquiry about giving radio talks to the BBC: 'I'm sorry', he said, 'Your voice is too sad.'

The baby monkey who was left tethered in the lab till Monday.

Clowns' convention: 'When you're a clown you can just do anything you like to people', he said. 'Lift them up, change everything round for them.'

Tess and friend go shopping for clothes, handbag on arm. They're ten.

Bibliography

Allen, C. K.: *Democracy and the Individual* (1943)

Dinnage, Rosemary: *Alone! Alone! Lives of Some Outsider Women* (2004)

Eisenbud, J.: *Psi and Psychoanalysis* (1970)

Fethney, Michael: *The Absurd and the Brave* (1990)

Kakar, Sudhir: *Shamans, Mystics and Doctors* (1983)

MacDonogh, G.: *A Good German,* (1992)

McDougall, Joyce: *Donald Winnicott the Man: Reflections and Recollections* (2003)

Shaw, George B.: *Intelligent Women's Guide to Socialism and Capitalism* (1928)

Schaeper, Thomas J. and Schaeper, Kathleen: *Cowboys into Gentlemen: Rhodes Scholars, Oxford, and the Creation of an American Elite* (1998)

Solomon, Andrew: *The Noonday Demon* (1998)

Winnicott, D. W.: *Playing & Reality* (1971)

Ziegler, Philip: *Legacy: Cecil Rhodes, The Rhodes Trust & Rhodes Scholarships* (2008)

Printed in Great Britain
by Amazon.co.uk, Ltd.,
Marston Gate.